Citizenship According to the Kingdom

A Life of Governmental Authority

Endorsements

Powerful teaching in the last great worldwide move of God taught us much about our rights, benefits and responsibilities in the family of God. My Friend, Greg Hood, in his new book, *Citizenship According to the Kingdom, A Life of Governmental Authority*, takes this to a powerful and much-needed new level! The insights in this book are game-changers. Every believer should read this book.

Dr. Dutch Sheets
Dutch Sheets Ministries and *Give Him 15* daily prayer and decrees. Bestselling author of: *Authority in Prayer, An Appeal to Heaven, Intercessory Prayer*
www.dutchsheets.org

My friend, Greg, has written a book empowered with great authority from our Father, bringing insight, revelation, and inspiration to equip each of us with the knowledge to live as sons and daughters of the Kingdom. It is more than a teaching manual; it is Holy Spirit breathed-upon, life-changing words. As you embrace them, meditate on them, and pray over them, you will walk in his freedom as a true citizen of his Kingdom, accomplishing his plans and purposes for your lives. Highly recommend.

Apostle Tim Sheets
Author of *Angel Armies, Angel Armies on Assignment, Planting the Heavens*
Tim Sheets Ministries
The Oasis Church, Middletown, Ohio www.timsheets.org

Citizenship According to the Kingdom

When Jesus died on the cross, he took our sin with him and left the concept of religion behind. Despite efforts to eliminate religion from our culture, some still strive to keep it alive. In recent years, I have come to believe that many in the Church have chosen to follow the rules of religion rather than seeking a genuine relationship with God. It's important to remember that only the sacrifice of Jesus can save us, not any religious actions.

However, the Lord did not stop at giving us his authority. He also granted us the power to become prophets, priests, and kings.

Throughout each chapter of this book, Greg Hood instructs us on how to manifest the Kingdom of God in our daily 9-to-5 lives here on the earth. He emphasizes that this goes beyond the walls of the church house. While many of us may not be five-fold ministers, it is still a part of a king's life to lead and guide others, to pray and prophesy for the benefit of the body, not because we consider ourselves superior or more holy, but because we have received the same care and guidance from others.

In addition to teaching us about citizenship, Greg also shows us how to be ambassadors for Christ and engage with the culture. His latest book, *Citizenship According to the Kingdom; A Life of Governmental Authority*, outlines how we can become influencers in the world. Although Greg has written other books on the Kingdom of God, this is his best work to date. I strongly recommend it as your next read.

Ricky Skaggs
15x Grammy Award Winner
Kentucky Music Hall of Fame – 2004
GMA Gospel Music Association Hall of Fame – 2012
Musicians Hall of Fame – 2016
The National Fiddler Hall of Fame – 2018
IBMA Bluegrass Music Hall of Fame – 2018
Country Music Hall of Fame - 2018

Endorsements

My friend Dr. Greg Hood's new book, *Citizenship According to the Kingdom: A Life of Governmental Authority*, will shift believers from an orphan mentality to a sonship identity; from serving religion to ruling and reigning in the Kingdom of God. It's a spirit-provoking read!

Jane Hamon
Co-apostle, Vision Church @Christian International
Author of *Dreams and Visions, Discernment, Declarations for Breakthrough, The Deborah Company* and *The Cyrus Decree*

My friend, Greg Hood, in his new work, *Citizenship According to the Kingdom; A Life of Governmental Authority*, challenges us to step up and take our place in God's kingdom purposes, especially in our roles in society and culture. In this present climate, where many Christian leaders are buying into the idea that we should just preach the gospel, Greg is showing us the other side of the coin. We are called, set and positioned by God to reclaim the foundations our nation was founded on, and our kingdom citizenship is step number one. Let this book stir you to do just that!

Robert Henderson
Best-Selling Author of the *Court of Heaven Series*

Dr. Greg Hood has done it again! He has written another excellent book concerning the prevailing theme of the Bible, i.e., the Kingdom of God.

He admirably weaves together the theological, cultural, political, and practical dimensions of being a citizen of God's present and eternal Kingdom. His explanation of the frequently misunderstood verse found in Philippians 3:20 impressed me: "For our citizenship is in heaven, from which we also eagerly wait for a Savior, the Lord Jesus Christ...." If the Body of Christ better understood this verse, they would not ignore their earthly citizenship responsibilities! How many times have we heard this statement by some followers of Jesus: "Politics is dirty, so don't get involved in cultural and political issues"? The apostle Paul knew and expressed his heavenly citizenship, but he also knew and exercised his Roman citizenship!

Greg explains how our heavenly citizenship calls us to responsibilities in our earthly citizenship. The main responsibility calls the Ekklesia-Church to be stewards and managers of the earth so that the will of God, which is always being done in heaven, will increasingly be done on earth. This was the flashpoint of the prayer the Lord Jesus taught His followers to pray. As intercessors, we pray this Jesus-taught model prayer. In addition, as ambassadors, we steward and manage the implementation of the will of God on the earth. This is how our heavenly citizenship informs and empowers our earthly citizenship!

Reading this very readable volume, I walked away feeling like an overcomer. This book had a sound to it. It was like the author picked up a megaphone and shouted "Victory! Victory for the purposes and plans of the Lord God in history and on the earth!"

I encourage you to read this informative and inspirational book for your own edification and to teach others the vital truth of an advancing and increasing Kingdom of God now in the earth.

The Kingdom of God does not lose in history! I love how Dr. Hood expresses it: "Kingdom citizens gauge their worth by their influence on the earth."

Dr. Jim Hodges
Federation of Ministers and Churches International Cedar Hill, TX

"Thy Kingdom come; Thy will be done, on earth as it is in heaven," will always be the will of God for his children. In order for this to become a reality in our lives, we must have a revelation and clarity concerning our dual citizenship. Dr. Greg Hood masterfully explains this reality in his new book, *Citizenship According to the Kingdom: A Life of Governmental Authority*. He brings us to the realization of the

Endorsements

truth that while we are in this world, we are not of it! We are citizens of another kingdom!

Isaac Pitre
Founder, Christ Nations Church 2Kings Global Network
Isaacpitre.org

I just finished perusing *Citizenship According to the Kingdom: A Life of Governmental Authority*. WOW! What a timely revelatory, prophetic book for today! I personally endorse this book as one of the most significant revelations for every five-fold minister; apostles, prophets, teachers, evangelists and pastors alike. This book is for every leader in the church and everyone who declares Jesus as Lord. Read it, practice it, and watch the power of God begin to flow through you—his gifted church—for his ultimate intentions. "The devil lost and God won." That will be the headlines in the next seasons.

Greg Hood has come as an apostle into the kingdom for this time. He's a man of prayer, he has apostolic power, and he's a leader among leaders. God bless all who read this book. It's a life changer.

Apostle Emanuele Cannistraci
Founding Pastor of GateWay City Church, San Jose, CA

Dr. Greg Hood is fast becoming the most prolific writer on biblical Kingdom Truth. This latest volume gives clear and sound guidance to all who will make the journey from membership to kingdom citizenship! This writing sets clear the awesome privileges of kingdom citizenship from start to finish. Jesus came to establish and release his kingdom on earth now!

Yes, there is more to come, yet our position as citizens and ambassadors is clear. This could be the first volume to read and embrace for believing Christians. I recommend it to all who are ready to be part of the victory!!!!

Dr. Ron Phillips, D.Min
Pastor Emeritus Abba's House, Chattanooga, TN
Fresh Oil Ministries

People arriving in the United States from other nations and desiring US citizenship go through a process. Greg Hood's powerful book, *Citizenship According to the Kingdom*, explains the process of becoming a citizen of the Kingdom of God. Understanding the rights, authority, government, influence, and other Kingdom characteristics shifts a person out of a religious mindset. The reader is challenged to arise and become a mature son or daughter of God. Greg's book should be a textbook for every Christian! All creation waits for Kingdom citizens to embrace their God-given destiny and fulfill God's great plan for Earth!

Barbara Wentroble
President, International Breakthrough Ministries
Author and Speaker

I am always excited when believers grasp their real identity and their true heavenly citizenship, which is why I am so pleased to recommend Greg Hood's book, *Citizenship According to the Kingdom*.

We cannot walk in freedom from sin or in power over the things of this world without knowing who we truly are, living in that divine and eternal dimension. I hope you will make time to read this book prayerfully and walk in your God-given identity for the rest of your life.

Joan Hunter, Evangelist
Host of Miracles Happen T V show
Joanhunter.org

I have known Dr. Greg Hood for over twenty years, and he has ministered at Word of Hope numerous times. I have personally

Endorsements

witnessed the remarkable anointing of the Holy Spirit in his life and ministry.

Dr. Hood's latest publication, *Citizenship According to the Kingdom; A Life of Governmental Authority*, offers valuable spiritual insights suitable for both new and seasoned believers. Given the current state of the world, the teaching in this book is more significant now than ever before. It will inspire you to deepen your relationship with God and become a more zealous ambassador for the Kingdom of God. I strongly recommend reading, studying, and putting into practice the principles contained within its pages.

Dr. David A Sobrepena, Word of Hope Church Manila, Philippines

As stated in Romans 8:14, "For all who are led by the Spirit of God, these are the sons of God." Therefore, it is crucial that we adopt the mindset of Christ as his sons and daughters. We have been granted citizenship in the Kingdom of God as children of the Most High King. When we pursue God wholeheartedly, we can have faith that his promises will come to fruition in our lives.

Dr. Greg Hood's latest book, *Citizenship According to the Kingdom; A Life of Governmental Authority*, highlights the significance of abiding by heaven's constitution: the Bible. It is essential for us, as children of God, to comprehend our covenant rights and live according to his word with confidence. By understanding and adhering to these priceless kingdom principles, we can live out God's promise as victorious citizens of his kingdom, just as Jesus promised. I encourage you to read this book and put its teachings into practice.

Congressman Josh Bercheen

Oklahoma's Second Congressional District, 118th Congress

Reading Dr. Greg Hood's new book, *Citizenship According to the Kingdom; A Life of Governmental Authority*, was an honor. It is a quick, easy-to-read book, a page-turner. It is written in Dr. Hood's very own conversational style. It is like you are sitting on your back porch having a substantive conversation with an old and truly knowledgeable friend, with his points all biblically based yet relatable.

Dr. Hood's take on many of the timeless issues of the day is delivered in a down-to-earth homespun fashion; the text starts off very lightly with observations on our culture and the meaning of citizenship. Then really gets to the significant part. The demonstrated biblical examples that undergird Dr. Hood's salient points are bulletproof. I can see how Greg's life experiences give him a unique perspective on our American culture and government.

I have seen Greg take public stands on behalf of morality and decency, and his motivation was to serve and honor God. This book is a road map for viewing contemporary moral challenges through the lens of timeless biblical wisdom. Not only does Greg talk the talk, but he also walks the walk! I recommend it with unbridled enthusiasm.

Bob McDermott (R), Hawaii State Representative 1996-2002, 2012-2022.
USMC Officer/ Desert Storm Veteran 1988-1992

I am personally grateful for the life and ministry of Dr. Greg Hood. Even to the most casual observer, it is obvious that Holy Spirit has anointed him for such a time as this. Once again, he has introduced a "working manual" on becoming kingdom-minded and kingdom-effective in this new book.

Dr. Hood's biblical encouragement to step into the fullness of the kingdom as a true citizen provides a mandate and a mantle as each of us fulfills the assignment that God has given to us. We have rights, we have authority, but more importantly, we have a relationship established by covenant. Dr. Hood effectively establishes the power of culture, influence, citizenship, and ambassadorship in this new book.

Endorsements

I highly recommend it for any believer at any level of maturity. I can't wait to get this into the hands of those that I shepherd. Well done, Greg, and thank you for your valuable kingdom investment into the Ekklesia.

Dr. Scott Reece
River City Church, Quad Cities

Dr. Greg Hood conveys in his book, *Citizenship According to the Kingdom; A Life of Governmental Authority*, the keys to understanding your sonship, citizenship and kingship in the kingdom of the Lord Jesus Christ. He outlines the knowledge and wisdom that must be administered to enable us to influence others into and through the Kingdom of God. By using your authority and power as a citizen, you will manifest divine power to lead in your assigned domains by embracing this truth.

Apostle Tony Kemp, President of ACTS GROUP
Tony Kemp Ministries

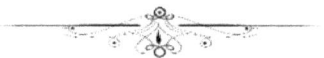

Dr. Greg Hood holds an authoritative mantle to train and equip believers in the ways of the kingdom. In this book, *Citizenship According to the Kingdom; A Life of Governmental Authority*, he has poured out research and revelation that will shift your mindset and activate you to operate as a citizen of the Kingdom of God. Within these pages, you can access great understanding and wisdom to see heaven on earth. Dr. Hood's writing will anchor your understanding and belief systems to God himself, drawing your revelation to foster a closer and more intimate relationship with Him.

Jeremy & Emily Bell
Kingdom Entrepreneurs
Dean at Kingdom University College of Business, Franklin TN

The call of God starts at the altar of salvation, but it leads to the altar of service. An army of recruits is only a loose collection of individuals until they look around and realize that they are together for a common purpose.

Historically, Christianity has focused on gathering the proverbial lost, thinking we were saving souls from hell. Today, we know that a greater effort is needed to fulfill Jesus' words: "On earth as it is in heaven." As Greg tells us: "Our great salvation starts as a rescue, continues as a restoration, and fully emerges as rights and responsibilities."

I often imagine the disciples staring at Jesus when he said: "Open your eyes and look at the fields! They are ripe for harvest."

Jesus' words echo through eternity. Our calling is as vast as our field of vision. How far are we willing to see? In *Citizenship According to the Kingdom*, Dr. Greg Hood challenges us to lift our eyes together, so see who we are in Christ—to see where we are in Christ—and to go forth into all the world as citizen-ambassadors of the Kingdom of God.

It is the clarion call that answers the eternal question: *Why am I here?*

Dr. Harold Eberle, Worldcast Ministries, Yakima WA
Author of numerous books, including *Father Son Theology*

Citizenship According to the Kingdom; A Life of Governmental Authority, is a compelling read for the times we are living in. While the world is reeling from a lost sense of personal and national identity, this book helps us identify who we are. Apostle Greg Hood has awakened in us the need to not only understand the Kingdom of God but also to know how to live and thrive in the Kingdom of God. I encourage you to digest this truth of citizenship from the perspective of the unseen world that we call the Kingdom of God. Apostle Greg masterfully unfolds the need and opportunity to live as a citizen of the

Endorsements

kingdom and to know your rights and authority as citizens of this continually revealed reality. By reading thoroughly through this book, you will be shocked as to how little we take advantage of being joint heirs in the domain of the Lord Jesus Christ. As one who travels through various borders of countries, I am aware there is favor and benefits towards one who is part of a country that has authority in the earth. You will want to take notes for yourself so you can refer to them from time to time to measure your growth in becoming aware of your position in the Kingdom of God.

Kerry Kirkwood, Senior Pastor
Trinity Fellowship Church, Tyler, Texas

At a time when many lines are blurred as to what is right or wrong, moral or amoral, Dr. Greg Hood's new book, *Citizenship According to the Kingdom; A Life of Governmental Authority*, brings a focused and insightful understanding of exactly what the Kingdom of God is, how it operates, and how we as followers of Jesus are to live within it. His definition of culture is especially important to why and how we walk out our purposes in God's plan and kingdom. From the first chapter to the last, this book will solidify the reality of God's kingdom in your mind and spirit. You have an important and powerful place in it. You won't wonder how the kingdom will affect this planet and its people.

Take the opportunity to read and reread this work until it is so strong in you that it can never be lost. Become the kingdom ambassador you were created to be. Take your stand as a member of God's Ekklesia. The Kingdom is waiting for the Sons and Daughters of the King to rise up as the true citizens they are, and this book will inspire you to be so and then show you how to do so. I'm sure you will find that while it is an awesome responsibility, it is also a thrilling way to live.

Dr. Bill Greenman
President, Global Purpose Strategies
Purpose International Consultants, LTD

Dr. Greg Hood has done it again! In this book, *Citizenship According to the Kingdom; A Life of Governmental Authority*, Dr. Hood illuminates the pathway to Kingdom living. This encouraging and disruptive teaching provides the wisdom and practical understanding we need to evolve into kingdom-minded people. Kingdom Citizenship is our most original and God-ordained position on the earth. Dr. Hood leads us into a new way of relating to and transforming the world through kingdom citizenship. This book is a must-have tool to create meaningful change in your own life and in the world around you.

Coach Scott Oatsvall
Health Coach, LT360Health.com

In my newest book, *Tribunals*, I write: Our passport identifies our citizenship. My passport clearly states that I am a citizen of the United States of America. In that passport, I have many stamps that have recorded all the countries that I have been in over the last several decades. I am using my third passport since they expire every ten years and, the other two were filled with stamps.

The passport is my identity. Even though, as I entered a foreign land, there was a period of time spanning several hours when I did not hold my United States passport in my hand, I still knew that I was a citizen of the United States; but I also knew that I had another passport. My United States passport declares that I am a citizen of this nation, but I also have another passport that is secured in heaven. It decrees that I am a citizen of heaven.

> *For our citizenship is in heaven, from which we also eagerly wait for a Savior, the Lord Jesus Christ; who will transform the body of our lowly condition into conformity with His glorious body, by the exertion of the power that He has even to subject all things to Himself.*
>
> Philippians 3:20-21

Endorsements

My friend Greg Hood once again clarifies our identity and the purpose of our identity in his newest book, *Citizenship According to the Kingdom; A Life of Governmental Authority*. He makes it very clear who owns our passport.

Dr. Tom Schlueter, Apostle
Texas Apostolic Prayer Network
Prince of Peace House of Prayer Arlington, Texas

I remember the first time I heard Greg Hood teach on *Citizenship According to the Kingdom*, and it was certainly an eye-opener. Even though I was raised in a Christian environment, I was somewhat surprised at what I heard. It didn't fit my paradigm or describe who I thought I was. I knew I was not a "sinner saved by grace." I knew my name was written in heaven, and that I had certain rights and responsibilities given to me by my heavenly Father. But comparing my earthly citizenship with my heavenly one brought the great revelation of my role, authority, and identity. Who we are is key to stepping into our authority, our rights, and privileges given to us by our Father God.

Greg Hood is an amazing teacher. He is not afraid to identify our sacred cows. It's up to us to put them on the altar. This book will give you the opportunity to examine your mindsets and come into the revelation of your rights and privileges as a citizen of the Kingdom.

Our King Jesus rules over a spiritual Kingdom, and we are his sons and daughters. We rule and reign with him now and in the hereafter. Read this book with a heart to step into your full stewardship, rights, and authority.

Regina Shank
Global Transformation International, www.reginashank.com

In a world filled with instabilities, crises, and chaos, it can sometimes seem impossible to maintain your peace. But in these despairing times, God will send His servants as a beacon of hope, and anoint them to deliver a message that destroys bondages and removes burdens from the lives of His people. I believe that Dr. Greg Hood is one of those servants, and *Citizenship According To The Kingdom* is that message.

This powerful message of the Kingdom is conveyed all throughout this book. And as you read, you will learn about the uniqueness of your Kingdom citizenship and the authority and power given you as such.

Just as God adequately equipped so many individuals throughout the Bible for the call upon their lives for such unique moments in history, God has also equipped you with everything you need for your "such a time as this." Be intimidated no more! They were vindicated and empowered to do exploits and so shall you be as you read this timely revelation of *Citizenship According To The Kingdom*!

Pastor Jennifer R. Biard, Lead Pastor
Jackson Revival Center Church, Jackson, MS

Citizenship According to the Kingdom

A Life of Governmental Authority

Greg Hood

Copyright

Citizenship According to the Kingdom
A Life of Governmental Authority
by Dr. Greg Hood, Th.D.

Copyright © 2023 by Greg Hood (Greg Hood Ministries/Ekklesia Publishing). All rights reserved. This book is protected by the copyright laws of the United States of America. This book may not be copied or reprinted for commercial gain or profit. The use of short quotations or occasional page copying for personal or group study is encouraged. Permission will be granted upon request from Greg Hood. All rights reserved. Any emphasis added to Scripture quotations is the author's own.

Unless otherwise noted, scripture quotations are taken from the New American Standard Bible, © 1960, 1962, 1963, 1968, 1971, 1972, 1973, 1975, 1977, 1995 by the Lockman Foundation.

Word studies in Greek, Hebrew and Aramaic are taken from:
- *Strong's Dictionary Concordance of the Bible, Greek and Hebrew.* James Strong LL.D., S.T.D. 1890
- *Brown-Driver-Briggs Hebrew and English Lexicon* © 2010 Snowball Publishing
- *Theological Dictionary of the New Testament* © 1985 William B. Eerdmans Publishing Company
- *AMG's Annotated Dictionary of the Old and New Testament* ©1984, 1990, 2008
- *The Complete Word Study Dictionary: Old Testament* by Warren Baker and Eugene Carpenter ©2003
- *The Complete Word Study Dictionary: New Testament* compiled by Spiros Zodhiates ©1992
- *The Peshitta Holy Bible Translated.* Translated from Aramaic ©2018 Lulu Publishing, 3rd edition ©2019

Edit/Layout by Jim Bryson (JamesLBryson@gmail.com)
Cover design by David Munoz (davidmunoznvtn@gmail.com)
Contact Info:
Dr. Greg Hood, Th.D.
Greg Hood Ministries / Kingdom University
1113 Murfreesboro Road
Suite 106 #222
Franklin, TN 37064
office@greghood.org, www.GregHood.org, www.KingdomU.org

Contents

Foreword .... - 1 -
Preface .... - 5 -
Introduction .... - 7 -
1. Citizenship .... - 11 -
2. Kingdom vs. Democracy .... - 23 -
3. Culture .... - 37 -
4. Ambassador .... - 75 -
5. Influence .... - 99 -
6. Boundaries .... - 113 -
7. Passport .... - 135 -
8. Uniqueness of Kingdom Citizenship .... - 155 -
9. Power of Humans .... - 167 -
10. Conclusion .... - 185 -
About the Author .... - 191 -
Previous Work .... - 193 -
Kingdom University .... - 205 -

Dedication

I DEDICATE THIS WORK to my beautiful wife and best friend, Joan Sobrepeña Hood, who walked through the tedious legal process of becoming a citizen of the United States of America. After some years as a green card holder, she was able to apply for citizenship in her new home country.

Joan, you are an amazing wife, mother, apostolic leader and woman of God. I know you will always be a Filipina in your heart and in your ways. I love that about you. You are a very valuable addition to this great nation we call home. You have also been used by Holy Spirit to help shape me to become the man I am today.

Thank you for loving Jesus more than you love me!

Acknowledgments

A VERY SPECIAL THANK YOU to Bishop Bill Hamon, who wrote the Foreword for this new work. I highly regard you, Sir, as a General in the faith and the father of the modern prophetic movement within the church. The ekklesia would not be as far along as she is without your tireless commitment to your assignment.

To all my friends and colleagues who gave endorsements for this book! Thank you! I am eternally grateful to those who gave me theological insight (and correction from time to time) for this work. You all have impacted my life in very special ways. I am thankful for our friendships.

A big thank you to my editor, Jim Bryson. Sir, you are a trooper! Thank you for staying in the trenches of this work to git 'er done. I also want to give a big shout out to Jacqueline Bryson. Thank you for all that you do behind the scenes. We all know Jim couldn't be the superhero that he is without you.

A special thank-you to Keith Long, Kathleen Bullock and Carrol McDonnell for all of your efforts in assisting with the proofreading. Thank you for catching all of my misspellings and grammatical mistakes.

Lastly, I want to thank all of our Kingdom University students, faculty, campus coordinators and host, as well as our staff, for all of your encouragement and for the "pulling" you often do to push me to dig deeper into research and the study of the Kingdom. This is an incredible life-changing journey that we are all on together.

Foreword

by Bishop Bill Hamon

I COUNT IT A PRIVILEGE to write the foreword for this book, *Citizenship According to the Kingdom*, by Dr. Greg Hood

The Apostle Peter declared that we should be established in the "present truth." According to God's plan and purpose for the restoration and destiny of the church, the proclamation of the Kingdom is the present truth for this day and prophetic time. Let me explain why this is true. My main ministry and writing have to do with restoration moves of God. Seven of my fifteen books deal with the origination, restoration and destiny of the Church.

We are in the Third Reformation. The First Reformation was the Church being birthed and spread to the ends of the Earth. The Second Reformation was the restoration of the Church which started in 1517 after the 1000 years Dark Age of the Church. There were nine major restoration movements in that 500-year period from 1517-2007. The basic gospel covers the death, burial, and resurrection of Jesus Christ. This Christian gospel could not be preached until the death and resurrection of Jesus and the birthing of the Church on the day of Pentecost. Jesus preached about the Kingdom over one hundred times in the four gospels. The Church was only mentioned once. Therefore, the Christian gospel couldn't be preached until the Church was birthed in 30 AD.

Citizenship According to the Kingdom

The Third Reformation began in 2008 after the Saint's Movement (the last restoration movement of the Church) finished restoring all New Testament truths back into the Church. These are truths which were lost during the 1000-year Dark Age.

In 1983, I had the vision for the restoration of the prophets and apostles being recognized as present day ministries in the Church. The prophetic movement was birthed in 1988.

In my book, *Apostles, Prophets and the Coming Moves of God*, (published in 1997), I proclaimed there would be three more moves of God before the second coming of Christ Jesus. The first was the Saints Movement which was birthed in 2007. The second was the Army of the Lord in 2016. The third and last movement will be the Kingdom Establishing Movement.

This is why Dr. Greg Hood's books on the Kingdom are present truth and relevant. Every move of God has taken a truth that Church theologians proclaimed was for the past or future, and made it experiential for today. It is now time to take the statement in the Lord's prayer from just personal blessings to end time prophetic purpose that is to take place during the Third Reformation.

Thy kingdom come
Thy will be done in earth
As it is in heaven.

The end result will be Revelation 11:15 which declares:

The kingdoms of this world are become the kingdoms of our Lord, and of his Christ; and he shall reign for ever and ever.

Every truth that has been spiritualized must be literalized. I am believing for revelation on how we fulfill that scripture and all those in the seventh chapter of the Book of Daniel. Maybe Greg's next book will contain revelation on how we, the Ekklesia, will be co-laborers with Christ Jesus in fulfilling the prophetic scripture in Rev 11:15.

Bless you, Greg, for your revelation and books on the Kingdom of God. It is evident that you are called to be a Third Reformation

Foreword

Reformer. Jesus birthed and built the Church to establish the Kingdom until His will is done on earth as it is in Heaven.

Bishop Bill Hamon

Bishop: Christian International Apostolic-Global Network

Author: *The Eternal Church, Prophets & Personal Prophecy, Prophets & the Prophetic Movement, Prophets, Pitfalls, & Principles, Apostles/Prophets & the Coming Moves of God, The Day of the Saints, Who Am I & Why Am I Here, The Final Reformation & Great Awaking, 70 Reasons for Speaking in Tongues, How Can These Things Be? God's Weapons of War, Your Highest Calling, The Final Reformation & Great Awakening*

Preface

WHAT IS THE FIRST THING that comes to mind when you hear the word *kingdom*? Sadly, (for many), the understanding of the word *kingdom* has been shaped by those who taught us, and that can be good or bad depending on the teacher's knowledge of how the Kingdom of God impacts our everyday life.

The idea of a kingdom is foreign to our Western mindset. For some, it can only be explained in terms of a bygone era where Sultans ruled over vast kingdoms filled with intrigue, riches, and cloaked in mystery that only a few have ever penetrated and lived to tell the tale.

A failure to grasp the meaning and measure of the kingdom has generated strife and division in the Body of Christ. It has led to denominational turf wars that still rage today. As the Apostle James warned, "My brethren, these things ought not to be so."

After four hundred years of silence, John the Baptizer came on the scene. He preached one message: "Repent, for the kingdom of heaven is at hand!" (Matthew 3:2). And, one chapter later, Jesus declared the same message. "From that time, Jesus began to preach and to say, 'Repent, for the kingdom of heaven is at hand'" (Matthew 4:17).

The significance of the message cannot be missed. Jesus did not come to declare a religion or even how to build the most prominent Church in town, but to declare God's rule and reign. Jack Taylor once said, "The good news is that there is salvation in the kingdom, but to dilute the message of the Gospel of Jesus to a mere plan of salvation dishonors the kingdom and does a huge disservice to the church. Jesus came preaching a kingdom, not just salvation. His message was on citizenship, not rescue."

It's time for our understanding to shift, not to what man thinks, but to what the Word of God teaches about the most crucial subject that one will ever know—the Kingdom of God!

What you hold in your hand is not just another book about the Kingdom of God. Apostle Greg Hood outlines clearly and undilutedly the aspects of the kingdom that must be defined and understood. He discusses various topics that many have minimized or ignored altogether. For instance, he outlines the importance of citizenship; the role of an ambassador; the boundaries of kingdoms; the uniqueness of kingdom citizenship; and so much more!

Apostle Greg's goal is clear-cut. He is determined to show the nature and expanse of the Kingdom of God and how it differentiates from all other ideologies, religions and political influences. When Jesus said, "But seek first the kingdom of God and His righteousness, and all these things shall be added to you," he told us that pursuing the kingdom must take priority over all other endeavors. (ref. Matthew 6:33).

Be prepared to explore aspects of the kingdom that might shift your religious paradigm into a new kingdom mindset that will radically change your life. As Apostle Greg says, "There is a God. He is our King. There is a kingdom. It's his. We call it the Kingdom of God. We are enrolled in his kingdom when we accept his rule and reign in our lives."

To which I say, GLORY!

Dr. J. Tod Zeiger
Friendsville, Tennessee 37737
www.todzeiger.com

Introduction

IN CHRISTIANITY, we often use common terms that we don't really understand, terms that we rarely take the time to define. This is because defining our terms takes effort. Yet until we agree on the meaning of a term, a phrase, a concept or a scripture, our application of these is useless. At best, they mean something to ourselves, but to the Body of Christ at large, we are merely one more bullfrog perched on our lily pad—one of millions floating in an infinite pond—filling our lungs with air and getting ready to croak.

Religion—man's empty attempts to codify the Christian experience—is rife with terms and concepts that it cannot define nor defend. The oft used phrase: "Well, it's a mystery," can only be supported with the fathomless expression: "Take it on faith."

I grew up in a religious environment and reached the age where I put religion to the test. In actuality, having been steeped in my denomination's doctrines, it was I who was being examined. The pursuit of truth begins, and remains, a personal journey. Mine started when I questioned terms like faith, salvation, and "living the good Christian life." Strange that everyone around me said these things— they even based their lives on these things—but no one could explain them to me in a way that made sense to this zealous teenager with a heart for God and a soul bound for trouble. Forty years later, armed with revelation that took me a lifetime to discover, I'm still bound for trouble—the best kind of trouble. The kind that shakes up people...and hell too! Glory to God!

It started with the development of a series of questions to help us get to the core meaning of scripture. Everything in Christianity ties back to scripture. It has to. All our dreams and suppositions, our experiences, our wisdom from trial and error—must relate back to something, somewhere in that holy book, as guided by God's Spirit.

The pursuit of truth begins, and remains, a personal journey.

Conventional Bible study, as conducted in the religious environment that I was raised in, approached the scriptures as something to be worshiped and adored but never questioned. The words printed on the page were sacred, even holy. The guiding principle for seeking truth was to apply no interpretation to scripture, but rather to glean the truth from God's Word itself without tainting it with "man's" viewpoint.

While that sounded noble, it only served to perpetuate the interpretation of a select few. In matters of controversy, of which there was a never-ending flow, we resorted to the interpretation of the venerable sages who had gone before us—those with reputation and titles, men ensconced in positions of prestige and power. By aligning with these esteemed individuals, we were assured protection from charges of heresy, rebellion, faithlessness or worse: of "being in the flesh!"

As a young firebrand, I knew religion was a powerless replica of the dynamic church Jesus spoke of in the New Testament, but I didn't know why it was powerless until I began to examine, not just what others say about scripture, but how we examine scripture in the first place. I began to uncover greater truth, and I realized why many are reluctant to undertake such a perilous journey.

When we challenge conventional thinking, especially that which purports to shield us from an eternity in hell, we encounter an unexpected vulnerability. People are herd animals. We value group identity over individuality. Standing up amidst the flock and declaring "We don't all have to be sheep!" can get you a prolonged time-out in

Introduction

the penalty box of the religious referees. So be it. Growing up in Mississippi, I never was good on ice anyway.

The first thing I uncovered is that everyone interprets the Bible. We have to. It's how we digest truth. We internalize it, break it down, apply it to our lives—remember, we will know the truth and the truth will set us free—and decide how close our present understanding takes us to the heart of God and his living Word.

In my book, *The Gospel of the Kingdom*, I developed some simple questions of inquiry to lead us in investigative thinking. I started with:

- Where are we?
- What are we doing?
- Why are we doing it?

To further understand scripture, I applied these four questions:

- Who said it?
- Who was it said to?
- What did it mean in that culture?
- How do we bring it into our lives?

I found that faithfully applying these questions led to some powerful, and at times, uncomfortable truth. Still, I was just getting started. I followed *The Gospel of the Kingdom* with *Sonship According to the Kingdom*. It was important not only to understand the gospel as Jesus presented it, but to understand our place in it. That place is family as sons and daughters of God.

With this present tome, *Citizenship According to the Kingdom*, I present our purpose and how that purpose is carried out. See, it's one thing to know what Jesus laid out, quite another thing to know who we are in that grand scheme. Until we appreciate our function in that scheme, we will remain as weak and ineffectual as the religious lot we deem powerless.

Our great salvation starts as a rescue, continues as a restoration, and fully emerges as rights and responsibilities. It is one thing to be healed; praise God for our healing through Jesus Christ of the sin condition that plagued our lives. It is a vastly different experience to evolve into a healer.

Folks, that is our true calling. Salvation is not just about who is going to heaven. Salvation isn't even about being "a King's kid." Salvation is a call to arms, for the righteous—those made so by the mercy and grace of God—to advance in the field of endeavor that aligns with our calling to establish the Kingdom of God. What is the Kingdom of God? It is wherever God is King.

> *Our great salvation starts as a rescue, continues as a restoration, and fully emerges as rights and responsibilities.*

Yes, kingdom starts in our individual lives, but it cannot remain there. We are saved; we are being saved; we will be saved. Now...change "we" to "they," and you have our purpose. It is only when we can look outwardly that we see the true meaning of what God is doing inwardly.

I invite you on a journey of discovery, one of destiny, not of yours alone, but that of mankind. It will require a few new definitions, some rattling of sacred concepts, the shaking of dusty comforters and scattering the moths. But one morning, as you look at that sleep-addled face that has dogged you since birth with the persistent questions: *Who am I? What am I doing? Why am I doing it?* You'll be able to answer:

We are the Kingdom of God!

1
Citizenship

Citizenship:

1. the status of being a citizen of a particular country;
2. membership in a community.

Merriam-Webster.com Dictionary

THE CLASSIC FILM, CASABLANCA, centers around the struggles of people fleeing the ravages of Nazi Germany during World War II. Because of the myriad of entry restrictions placed on foreign passport holders, a deliberate route through a maze of neutral countries was required to gain access to the free countries of the West. Each country—each step of the way—offered a measure of safe passage. It was not until the refugee finally landed on the bonny shores of a Western country that they could breathe free.

In modern times, an effort was made to unite the various countries of Europe. Thus, the European Union was formed. Now, I know that some folks feared this event as the heralding of the dreaded "one-world government" and the reign of Big Foot (or the Anti-Christ, or whatever your eschatology supports.) But one thing is for certain. The unification of Europe has made travel and subsequent trade much easier, and with it the flow of the gospel. Travelers who used to dread border crossings now find themselves and their message flowing with relative ease under the citizenship of a common passport and currency.

Indeed, we can look back approximately 75 years to the formation of NATO and the promise of a united front to face the threat of hostile nations. Nations that at various times found themselves at odds over territory, tariffs, and secret alliances found greater strength and security in a common purpose and assured support.

Throughout scripture, the tribes, cities and nations of Israel sought to be unified under family headship, tribal law, the rule of prophets and judges, and kingdom. Remarkably, kingdom was not God's first choice, at least, not the way the people wanted it. They wanted a human king. God wanted to be their king. Still, the people's desire indicated the sense of security, status and purpose that comes from belonging to a kingdom.

> *Gradually, the sturdy planks of a once stable and productive society are being reduced to splinters by salvo after salvo fired from the cannons of the enlightened mob.*

We call that belonging *citizenship.* It was an important status in Bible days, and it is important today. In fact, more so today as our world—the same world that God so loved—fragments under the onslaught of identity politics. We are no longer merely human beings. We are no longer Americans, French, Brazilians or North Pole-ians. We are not simply white, black, red, yellow or brown. We are no longer men or women, but 67 varieties of gender dystopia delineated by people who can't figure out which bathroom to use. We are divided by blue state, red state, pro-this or pro-that depending on which newsfeed is supplying us sound bites. Gradually, the sturdy planks of a once stable and productive society are being reduced to splinters by salvo after salvo fired from the cannons of the enlightened mob. We are being

Citizenship

reduced piles of kindling, waiting...even dreading...that one fateful match that could torch it all.

Unless....

Unless we realize that under the blue domed sky, we are all creatures of the Creator, subject to him; there is little to fight over, little to divide us, and everything to unite us. It is no wonder that every nefarious scheme of the enemy includes the removal of God—be it atheism or religion—to foist its will on mankind. In this, however, the enemy tips his hand. If you have to convince me that my Father doesn't exist before you try to take me down, I gotta wonder: Who are you afraid of?

There is an answer to our present-day challenges. It's been there all along, and the plethora of deceptions only serves to divert our attention from its existence. Truth is truth. Always has been. Always will be. "A" is "A."

There is a God. He is our King. There is a kingdom. It's his. We call it the Kingdom of God. We are enrolled in his kingdom when we accept his rule and reign in our lives—when we become citizens.

> *Truth is truth. Always has been. Always will be. "A" is "A."*

In the coming pages, we are going to learn what it means to be a citizen of the Kingdom of God. Folks, the reason Satan's schemes to divide mankind have worked so well is that we have not looked high enough for our identity. Nothing wrong with calling ourselves men or women, Southern or Northern, Steelers or 49'ers. (I'm drawing the line at Cowboys.) The problem is that we are not reaching for heaven. All identity—and all blessing—flows from God above. He's called Father for a reason. He is the Source. The Absolute. The "A."

It behooves us to learn what it means to be a citizen of the kingdom. Benefits go both ways, don't they? Let's start with answering the age-old question: "What's in it for us?"

Well...everything, more or less.

CARE

In a kingdom—assuming it is a benevolent kingdom—it is the king's responsibility to care for his citizens. A king's worth is gauged by how well his citizens live—the quality of their lives. Now, I'm not just talking about money or big houses or fancy chariots (though one with mud flaps and a lift kit would be cool). Kingdom citizens gauge their worth by their influence on the earth.

From the Old Testament, we know that Solomon was the richest man of his day. He was the Elon Musk of the burning sands. But it wasn't so much Solomon's lifestyle that affected people like the Queen of Sheba. When she visited him, she brought as many gifts as she could think of to impress this Sultan of Swag. In those days, influence was everything. (In our modern times, influence is still everything, but hold the olive oil and fig cakes.) When kings give gifts to other kings, they didn't do so to bless them. They did so to impress them. (ref. 1 Kings 10.)

There is a jungle tribe near the equator that decides individual status based on who can take the biggest hit with a club. Upon meeting, each warrior takes a swing at the cranial of the other with a hardened weapon of dense wood. This goes back and forth until only one man is left standing. (Or the other guy runs out of blood or develops a severe case of mental retardation.)

When the Queen of Sheba brought gold, spices and precious stones, she was hoping to knock Solomon off his throne, so to speak. This would give her the status she needed to dictate terms in any future alliances and disputes. Unfortunately for her, it didn't work out that way. The Bible says she was overwhelmed by Solomon's palace, the food of his table, even the array of his court. Feeling faint, she nearly fainted in awe of the quality of life that even Solomon's servants had, a level that rivaled her personal lifestyle.

> *When the queen of Sheba saw all the wisdom of Solomon, and the house that he had built, and the food of his table, the seating of his servants, the service of his waiters and*

their attire, his cupbearers, and his burnt offerings which he offered at the house of the Lord, she was breathless.

1 Kings 10:4

Now, translate that into our life with our King. We are told that she presented her gifts to Solomon, yet she left with everything she asked for.

And King Solomon granted the queen of Sheba everything she desired, whatever she requested, besides what he gave her in proportion to his royal bounty. Then she departed and went to her own land together with her servants.

1 Kings 10:13

Why? Simple math. Solomon, as the preeminent king of the known world, could not allow her to outgive him. This was especially crucial considering that his rule was a theocracy. His position, power and prestige were derived from God, the King of the king.

But as interesting as this story is, something happened between "Here, King," and "Wow!" The Queen of Sheba had an epiphany, (which is a fancy way of saying "the light came on"). She blessed God.

Here is what happened:

But I did not believe the stories until I came and my own eyes saw it all. And behold, the half of it was not reported to me. You have exceeded in wisdom and prosperity the report which I heard. Blessed are your men, and blessed are these servants of yours who stand before you continually and hear your wisdom! <u>Blessed be the Lord your God</u> who delighted in you to put you on the throne of Israel; because the Lord loves Israel forever, He made you king, to do justice and righteousness."

1 King 10:7-9

Notice the order of events. She came to impress. Instead, she was impressed beyond her wildest imagination. She honored God as the source of what she saw. She departed even more blessed than when she came. Solomon's influence won her over. Not his riches, not his good looks, not his wisdom...but the source of all of these things. She arrived a material girl. She departed a spiritual girl.

GOD'S PROVISION

This same king rules our lives today if we submit to his rule. It is his nature that he will not allow us to outgive him, as long as we honor him. When we bring offerings to him—when we serve in his kingdom—he will make sure we go home with more than we brought, especially when his provision further feeds the assignment for our lives.

Poverty is not the goal. Abundance is not the goal. Knowing the provider is the goal, and abundance is the result. The difference is the process that transforms us from a poverty mindset into a prosperity mindset. God is a good giver. He looks for excuses to bless us. Our willingness to give and acknowledge him as the giver is all the reason God needs to overwhelm us with his goodness.

Nowhere in the Bible does it say that God gets glory out of our being poor. Yes, religion tells us that poverty is honorable, even holy. Since when does religion track with the Spirit flowing from God's heart? Poverty is not holiness; it just means our pockets are full of holes. Amen!

> *Poverty is not the goal. Abundance is not the goal. Knowing the provider is the goal, and abundance is the result.*

God wants to give us everything we need for our assignment, and he wants us to have it now. However, there are reasons why we don't get it now. Those reasons start with the face we see above the bathroom sink every morning.

There are things we are delayed from doing because we don't have the resources to do them. Yet we know God wants us to have them; indeed, we need them to fulfill our purposes. And so, we look at our lives squarely and say, "God, what is it that is holding these things back? Why am I not fulfilling your calling on my life?"

Well, it's not God. Right? It's us. It's a matter of aligning our lives with him. It's not our ability to do great things. It's our ability (read: *maturity*) to steward what he puts in our hands, because everything he gives us contains a seed. Oh sure, it may look like a harvest to us. It may be something bigger than we have ever received in life. But buried deep within it is something to sow. God is saying "Plant it. Don't eat it. Use it to enlarge your tents."

Joan and I sometimes look at things that God has brought into our lives, and we think, "Man, this is an amazing harvest." Then I hear the Lord say, "No, it is the seed for things beyond amazing; for things you cannot even imagine yet."

Every harvest produces seed. That's how God's blessings perpetuate themselves. If all we see is the bounty, we will not be willing to make the sacrifice to sow some—if not all—for another season.

The religious mindset says to consume it. Eat it all. God has unlimited supply, right? And when it's time to sow, the seed will just appear. Presto!

Yeah...no. That's not how it works. God is maturing us. We are being taught discipline. A dollar is still worth 100 cents, whether it's in the hands of a beggar or Jeff Bezos. We need to value it as such. The fact is, God has everything; we don't. Specifically, we lack the maturity to handle greater blessings until we grow into them.

Greater blessing always contains more seed to sow for more blessing to enter our lives. That is why the tithe is a percentage, a tenth (10%) of the whole. It's not a finite quantity like fifty *omers* of wheat or ten cows. (What is an *omer*, anyway?) The tithe, like all sowing, is the harvest working for us. Of course, we consume some of the harvest because we need it. But we also distribute it wherever God has called us to operate.

Citizenship According to the Kingdom

Kingdom life is a life of faith, a life of fulfillment. Citizenship is a life based on God's promise that he will take care of everything we need. Religion teaches us the mechanics of the kingdom—the metaphysics, if you will—but it negates the relationship with God. The kingdom has laws, but religion co-opts these into rules that we must adhere to in the hopes of persuading God to bless us.

- If I do this, God will give me that.
- If I say all the right things, all the right things will appear.
- If I do unto others, the same will happen unto me.
- If I act in a good way, then maybe God will let me have what I need to work for him.

More times than not, however, these things work to an extent. This is because religion's rules are based on God's laws. However, religion misses the reason for the laws in the first place. God wants people who seek him for *who he is*, not for *what he gives*. God's giving is to teach us to receive, to steward, and to grow into fully-vested sons and daughters of the King.

Citizenship is a life based on God's promise that he will take care of everything we need.

Religion will have us doing all the right things for all the wrong reasons. And who knows...we might just get that gold-plated Rolls Royce we've been believing for, but we'll be no closer to God than when we drove a Pinto. And now we have this behemoth to maintain. (The oil changes alone will bankrupt us.)

Receiving from God is not a matter of bending his heart. He already loves us enough to have sent his son. The Father already has everything we need in his treasury. What, then, do we need to do to receive? We need to come into alignment with him, his plan, and his purpose. We cannot remain children possessed of a slave mentality seeking to meet our needs. Sons and daughters know what is theirs. We share the family heritage. We are citizens by rebirth.

Citizenship

> *Receiving from God is not a matter of bending his heart. He already loves us enough to have sent his son.*

Now, we do not give based on needs. Giving to someone or something based on their lack is something we should rarely do. We should give to the vision. Our giving should say, "I believe in you. I align with what you are doing. I see good things happening here. May this gift yield even greater things."

Yes, visions have needs, but our seed is not going into the vision if the mentality is, "Oh dear, they don't have enough to do it. They can't make it happen. They can't get it done."

When we sow into lack, we reap lack. No, we are to sow into life, taking some of our life and putting it into the vision so that we harvest life. We do give to the poor, but not because they are poor. We sow into the poor, believing for great things for them.

> *One who is gracious to a poor person lends to the LORD, And He will repay him for his good deed.*
>
> Proverbs 19:17

God says when we give to the poor, we lend to him. And he gives it back to us. He repays it back to us. Why? So that we can sow even more. The day we find ourselves sitting fat, dumb and happy on a pile of grain, merrily eating away our seed, is the day we eat our way into poverty.

When we give to the poor, God repays it. There is no way to twist the scriptures to say we are getting interest on our money. It simply means a return for what we lent.

> *Give, and it will be given to you. A good measure, pressed down, shaken together and running over, will be poured into your lap. For with the measure you use, it will be measured to you.*
>
> Luke 6:38

> *The day we find ourselves sitting fat, dumb and happy on a pile of grain, merrily eating away our seed, is the day we eat our way into poverty.*

Now, when we are sowing and giving into a vision, God tells us that we can expect a harvest. Why? Because we are allowing that vision to grow, and as we do, our investment produces a harvest back into our lives. That is the true principle of sowing and reaping versus merely giving to the poor.

From a kingdom perspective, where we put our resources is where we put God. Indeed, our resources are not ours; not really. We are stewarding our resources for God. To the extent that we invest where God says to invest, we can expect a great return. But if we invest somewhere else—perhaps motivated by pity, greed, or ignorance—we will answer to Father. The good news is that God rarely punishes. He almost always educates. Failure is simply an indication of the need.

WHO ARE WE?

As Kingdom citizens, it is important to understand that our lives are not our own. We belong to the King. As Paul told us:

> *I have been crucified with Christ and I no longer live, but Christ lives in me. The life I now live in the body, I live by faith in the Son of God, who loved me and gave himself for me.*
>
> Galatians 2:20

So, if our lives belong to God, what does that make us? It makes us citizens.

> *So, then you are no longer strangers and foreigners, but you are fellow citizens with the saints, and are of God's household,*
>
> Ephesians 2:19

Citizenship

For our citizenship is in heaven, from which we also eagerly wait for a Savior, the Lord Jesus Christ;

Philippians 3:20

A citizen is a member of a state or nation. But there is a further distinction to our alliance, that of ambassador.

Therefore, we are ambassadors for Christ, as though God were making an appeal through us; we beg you on behalf of Christ, be reconciled to God.

2 Corinthians 5:20

...and pray in my behalf, that speech may be given to me in the opening of my mouth, to make known with boldness the mystery of the gospel, for which I am an ambassador in chains; that in proclaiming it I may speak boldly, as I ought to speak.

Ephesians 6:19-20

We need to understand that when Paul uses terms like citizen, citizenship, and ambassador. These are not religious terms. These are governmental terms. Just as citizenship in our home country has nothing to do with our religion, so our citizenship in the Kingdom of God has nothing to do with religion. Citizenship pertains to our rights and responsibilities that we have as citizens of our nation. It calls us to be a member of that nation.

In the United States, we have natural-born citizens and naturalized citizens. Ironically, the naturalized citizens face a tougher process to becoming citizens. All natural-born citizens have to do is be born within the legal jurisdiction of the United States. Although that can be a difficult task in and of itself.

My wife, Joan, who is from the Philippines, had to take classes and pass a test to become a U.S. Citizen. One of the proudest moments of my life was watching Joan stand up with a flag in her left hand and her right hand raised as she pledged her life to protect the Constitution of the United States against all enemies, foreign and domestic. (I wonder how many natural-born citizens would be willing to do the same today.)

Joan took the same oath that our military and our elected officials take. Naturalized citizens pledge to love our country, to submit to its laws, to ingrain themselves in this country, to make America their nation, to protect it and stand for it. These are things that we as citizens often take for granted. When the process is complete, naturalized citizens have the same rights as natural-born citizens. (The only exception being they cannot be President. That requires natural-born citizenship.)

Many of our grandparents or great-grandparents experienced the same naturalization process. They came through Ellis Island and other ports of entry, saying, "We want to be American. We want to be a part of the American dream. We want to be a part of what America can provide, and we want to contribute."

They are the reason that many of us today were born citizens. Citizenship is an awesome thing. A person owes allegiance to a government, and that allegiance entitles them to protection and provision. A kingdom is a form of government, one in which a king provides for them. It is the king's responsibility to make sure his citizens are well taken care of, that they have opportunity to make a living.

There was a time in history, even in our lifetime, that the British empire spread itself across the globe. Hence, the saying: "The sun never sets on the British empire." The sun was always shining somewhere in that kingdom. It may have been dark in Mother England, but in Hong Kong or India—territories of Great Britain—the sun was burning in all its glory.

We must understand that the Kingdom of God shines with eternal glory. Ultimately, we are not citizens of an earthly kingdom. Ours is a heavenly realm, both in what is available to us and what is required of us.

2

Kingdom vs. Democracy

A KINGDOM AND A DEMOCRACY share similar traits and striking differences. We will look at a few of the differences here in this chapter.

PROTECTION

A king provides protection. What does that look like as citizens of the Kingdom of God? For starters, there is an army. Every kingdom has an army, and the citizens of that kingdom are protected by that army. Well, the army of God's kingdom are the angels. It is not us. We are not the army of God. We are kings. Angels comprise the army of God. We lead the army.

When the enemy looks at us on the battlefield, he doesn't see privates, corporals, sergeants, majors, or generals. He sees kings. He doesn't see us ranked among ourselves. He sees all of us with crowns on our heads, kings arrayed against him. Imagine what the enemy feels when an army of kings come after him—kings charging, swords drawn, leading a host of angels to take a territory for God.

Religion tells us we are the army of God, that we are fighting for God. But like most things in religion, that is incorrect. We lead the army of God. That is why our position on the battlefield is so important. If you go onto the battlefield and think that you are only ranked a private and these other people are master sergeants, second lieutenants, colonels, and generals, then you'll think you are less than what those other people are. Subconsciously, you might even use it as an excuse to not perform at the same level. But if we all go on the battlefield crowned as kings, then we are all ranked together. Nobody is thinking: *Well, they're greater than I.* Or: *I am the greatest...next to that guy...who is lower than that guy.* Certainly, some people have more experience than we do, but we don't have any less authority than anyone else standing beside us. In this Kingdom mindset as sons and daughters of the king, we all go to battle carrying the same level of authority. Our giftings and callings as fivefold ministers may give us different positionings—they may allow us to lead other kings—but it doesn't mean that those we lead are less than we are just because we are apostles or prophets or authors. (God help us all).

Hierarchal thinking is religious thinking. In the Kingdom of God, we are called to serve the Body of Christ. As leaders, we are to enhance its capabilities. We are to teach, to guide, to pioneer, and to position others to conquer battles the same way we do. And hopefully, they will do it better.

PROVISION

Jesus had a lot to say to his disciples—the future stewards of the Kingdom of God on earth—regarding God's provision for them and their attitudes towards it.

> *Hierarchal thinking is religious thinking.*

For this reason, I say to you, do not be worried about your life, as to what you will eat or what you will drink; nor for your body, as to what you will put on. Is life not more than food, and the body more than clothing? Look at the birds of the sky, that they do not sow, nor reap, nor gather crops into barns, and yet your heavenly Father feeds them. Are you not much more important than they? And which of you by worrying can add a single day to his life's span? And why are you worried about clothing? Notice how the lilies of the field grow; they do not labor nor do they spin thread for cloth, yet I say to you that not even Solomon in all his glory clothed himself like one of these. But if God so clothes the grass of the field, which is alive today and tomorrow is thrown into the furnace, will He not much more clothe you? You of little faith! Do not worry then, saying, 'What are we to eat?' or 'What are we to drink?' or 'What are we to wear for clothing?' For the Gentiles eagerly seek all these things; for your heavenly Father knows that you need all these things. But seek first His kingdom and His righteousness, and all these things will be provided to you.

So do not worry about tomorrow; for tomorrow will worry about itself. Each day has enough trouble of its own.

Matthew 6:25-34

Jesus' message was clear. "Do not take concern for your own life." Why? That is his responsibility. It is God's responsibility to provide for us. It is his responsibility to feed us and to clothe us. Let your heart rejoice in that truth.

> *So do not worry about tomorrow; for tomorrow will worry about itself.*

Of course, one might interpret this by saying: "Well, Greg, that sounds wonderful. I don't want to work. I want to bang on the drum all day. And come evening tide, I'll be at your house. What time's dinner?"

Quite the contrary. We are supposed to be moving in what the Father has assigned us to do. We are taking the Kingdom of God everywhere we go. Often, our most productive mission field is the workplace. When we walk in the will of God, God's will walks in us. He manifests everything that he needs in our lives. That includes jobs—the means to earn a living.

But you are to remember the Lord your God, for it is He who is giving you power to make wealth, in order to confirm His covenant which He swore to your fathers, as it is this day.

Deuteronomy 8:18

Our Father is not a deadbeat or absentee dad. As David tells us:

God is our refuge and strength,
A very ready help in trouble.

Psalm 46:1

The Father never leaves us; he never forsakes us.

Be strong and courageous, do not be afraid or in dread of them, for the Lord your God is the One who is going with you. He will not desert you or abandon you.

Deuteronomy 31:6

...and behold, I [Jesus] am with you always, to the end of the age.

Matthew 28:20

If Father gives you an assignment—if he moves you to do something—do not be moved by what you see. Be moved by the assignment. That is faith, to see what God sees.

...God, who gives life to the dead and calls into being things that do not exist.

Romans 4:17

If we judge what we need to do in life by what we see and feel—if we merely react to what is going on around us—we are going to miss the deeper walk with God. We will not follow through with the greater things God has for us to do because we are focused on the immediate needs: food, clothing, shelter, and the storms of life, be they weather, politics or relationships. Folks, there is nothing wrong with feeding your families, mowing your lawns, or voting the bums out of office so the next bums can take their place. The problems come when everyday life becomes our sole focus. Consider these scriptures.

True spirituality that is pure in the eyes of our Father God is to make a difference in the lives of the orphans, and widows in their troubles, and to refuse to be corrupted by the world's values.

James 1:27 TPT

Truly, truly I [Jesus] say to you, the one who believes in Me, the works that I do, he will do also; and greater works than these he will do; because I am going to the Father.

John 14:12

We are called to both the natural and the supernatural. Neither is less than the other. We serve a powerful God. He fills the bellies of the hungry, and he moves nations to receive the glory of his kingdom. There is nothing that can withstand him...or us when we are aligned with him.

And behold, a violent storm developed on the sea, so that the boat was being covered by the waves; but Jesus Himself was asleep. And they came to Him and woke Him, saying, "Save us, Lord; we are perishing!" He said to them, "Why are you afraid, you men of little faith?" Then He got up and rebuked the winds and the sea, and it became perfectly calm. The men were amazed, and said, "What kind of a man is this, that even the winds and the sea obey Him?"

Matthew 8:24-27

These things I have spoken to you so that in Me you may have peace. In the world you have tribulation, but take courage; I have overcome the world."

John 16:33

Be of good cheer. Take courage. When God gives you an assignment and all you see are obstacles, push beyond them. Why?

Because it is God's responsibility to feed you, clothe you, shelter you, and bring everything into your life that you need to complete that assignment.

When God leads us in faith journeys and we are not seeing things manifest, that doesn't mean they are not going to show up when they are needed. There have been times when Joan and I have heard God say, "Do these conferences," or "Do these meetings," or "Go to this nation." Our hearts say "Yes" but our checkbook says, "Are you crazy?!" Yet we stand in faith. "Praise God, we are going. Come on, checkbook. Learn something about the provision of God."

> *Be of good cheer. Take courage. When God gives you an assignment and all you see are obstacles, push beyond them.*

The natural part of us can only see the zeros in our bank account. That's the logic side; the responsible side. Nothing wrong with that side of us. But the faith part of us sees the one—the mighty one—in front of all those zeros. (It's the number of 0s after the 1 that determines the amount.)

Our hearts turn to God, and we take courage. We know that when there is a lack, God is getting ready to reveal his abundance. So, we respond to God, make plans to visit certain nations, and the Lord supernaturally brings us the finances that we need to go.

Certainly, there are times when we have enough to do what we are called to do. We have plenty and are able to take people with us. Those are no less godly. But other times, the Lord says, "I want you to start planning; I want you to announce it; I want you to do it."

"But Lord, there's no money."

"I want you to announce it; I want you to plan it; I want you to do it."

"Okay, Lord. I get the message. You are getting ready to do some good here. Thank you."

Over the years, we have learned not to even question the Lord, just go for it. And he provides. Even if his provision shows up at the last minute, even if it is after the event and we have had to sweat and pray, laying on the floor and sucking the carpet. That is good too. We probably needed to build our faith, and the carpet needed cleaning anyway. We know that whenever we are moving in his assignment, the Father is faithful.

Although God promises to comfort us, his focus is not our comfort. It can easily lull us into a false sense of complacency. We want things easy. We want them to just flow. Well, sometimes it does; sometimes it doesn't. When we are taking new territory, devils do not give up without a fight. We need to adjust our strategy accordingly. Diplomacy doesn't work with the enemy. We just need to invade. We need to move in and say, "Get out! You are in my seat. That's marked for God's kingdom."

This can't be mere verbiage. It can't just be a positive confession. We have to carry the weight of it. It requires a knowing within our spirit that Father is partnering with us and we are partnering with him. As we do our part as sons and daughters who walk in his authority, Father releases his part. We are citizens of his kingdom. Nothing can change that.

Religion can't operate this way. Religion needs boards of directors, committees, budgets, and fundraisers. Religion needs all of these campaigns to be done to make sure the resources are in the bank before anything is started. Religious people love the phrase "count the cost" from Luke 4:28, yet they fail to make the connection to God's truth. "Count the cost" doesn't mean count our pennies and decide if we are going to obey God or not. It means count the cost to our present way of living. The cost of obeying God is in the shift from self-sufficiency to God-sufficiency. It is releasing our resources in return for his resources. It is going from our limited means to God's endless provision. It is stepping out in the full understand of who we are, and whose we are: citizens of God's kingdom.

In the Kingdom, Father's treasuries are always full. We make withdrawals, but they are drawn on heaven's bank. Often, people approach Joan and me and say, "I want to give you this. You have something you want to do. I want you to take it."

We look and it's a check with too many zeros to count. It takes two checks stapled together just to write the number. This boggles our minds, and we both start crying, thanking the Lord: "You are so awesome, God."

> *The cost of obeying God is in the shift from self-sufficiency to God-sufficiency.*

We know the provision is not for us; it is for the assignment. We don't have the pleasure or the privilege of partaking of it. We put everything into the assignment and are faithful with it. We do not use it to pay the electric bill or the car payment or go out to eat. We know that gifts like that are for the assignment. Often, it meets our expenses down to the penny.

Folks, God is good. Do not worry. Do not be concerned about your lives. You are not your own. It is Christ that is living in you. All things are possible. All things are made new.

ASSIGNMENT VISION

As of this writing, there is an excitement swelling up in me about the state of Tennessee where Joan and I live. More than a residence, we have an assignment here. God has placed us here to have a voice in the city, the region and the nation. It is a voice of authority; it's a voice of resolve coming from a place of right standing in God. We have learned that whenever God gives us those things, it is not for our comfort. It is for our influence.

There is an anticipation stirring in me for Tennessee that I don't know how to put in words yet. God is getting ready to set the hills of Tennessee on fire with his glory. I had a vision one night. (I dream often.) I saw little pockets of fire all over the hills of Tennessee. And in my natural mind, I reverted back to documentaries, pictures, and movies, and thought, "Oh, those are moonshiners. They've got the hills lit up."

The Spirit of the Lord said, "No, that's my son setting fires as he walks through this state."

The Lord was walking through the state of Tennessee, and in every place that his foot touched down, a fire was lit. Glory!

This has nothing to do with religion. It is about taking the territory of Tennessee, bringing it back into the Kingdom of God as the first fruits of what God is doing in this nation. I am excited to see what God is doing in Tennessee.

When you go forward in what God has called you to do, you need to have the vision within you for the region. Kingdom is about spreading God's influence in our communities, cities, regions, and nations. It is about taking territory. It is not about plundering hell to populate heaven. That was a popular saying back in the charismatic days. Well, hell doesn't need plundering. Jesus already owns hell. He is the Lord over hell, not the devil. As citizens of the Kingdom of God, we inhabit territory that was previously owned by other kings.

CITIZENSHIP COMES WITH RIGHTS

> *Kingdom is about spreading God's influence in our communities, cities, regions, and nations.*

As Americans—whether natural born or naturalized, we exercise the rights of citizens of the United States of America. The same is true of citizens of the Kingdom of God. In a kingdom, we live by rights. We live our lives through these rights, not through some mystical magical miracle that God may do for us from time to time.

We don't have to feel like an American to be an American. Sometimes I don't feel like an American when I see what is happening in our country, but I still am a citizen. Why? My birth certificate and passport say I am an American. I have the rights of this nation. I get to vote, not because I feel like voting but because it is my right as a United States citizen to vote. Non-citizens do not have that right. When Joan carried a green card before she became a naturalized citizen of the United States, she had almost all the privileges that I had as a citizen, except she could not vote. She could not decide who in our nation was in authority and power. That right belongs to citizens.

OUR CONSTITUTION ESTABLISHES OUR RIGHTS

All the rights that you and I have are established by the Constitution of the United States, including the Bill of Rights, which is the first 10 Amendments of the Constitution. It spells out Americans' rights in relation to their government—things we have as citizens that we can expect the government to enforce for us. They are inherent to us because we are citizens.

The Constitution is not a religious document. It is a governmental declaration that God sponsored to give us certain inalienable rights. We live and depend on the rights stated by that document.

Similarly, as citizens of the Kingdom of God, our constitution is the written Word of God—the Bible. Throughout its pages, God recorded all we needed to live according to his will. It spells out our rights and responsibilities as citizens of the kingdom, including the things we can expect God's government to enforce for us.

CITIZENS IN THE KINGDOM OF GOD LIVE BY RIGHTS

What are some of the rights that we have as citizens of the Kingdom of God? What are some of the things that have been purchased? What are some of the things that have been taken on our behalf? What are some of the things that have been established?

We have a right to physical healing. It is a right, not a happenstance. It's not a random thing where God's in a good mood one day and feels like healing certain people. Hear me: We have healing in our nation, the Kingdom of God, because it is an inherent right as citizens. This is our healthcare plan. Not Blue Cross-Blue Shield. It's the Red Cross of Christ. Hallelujah. When we fully understand our rights, we don't ask God to heal us; we already have healing as citizens. It is God's responsibility to provide that for us.

Now, writing like this can make people a little nervous because it sounds like I'm saying we can put a demand on God. Well shucks...you got me. Absolutely we can put a demand on God! Why? Because God said, "You can put this demand on me. As your King, I am guaranteeing you a right to healing. By Jesus' stripes, you *were* healed." In fact, he said it twice!

And by His wounds we are healed.

Isaiah 53:5

By His wounds you were healed.

I Peter 2:24

Jesus bought healing for the Body of Christ and made it a part of our culture of the Kingdom of God. That right to healing belongs to us. When we lay hands on someone who is sick, we are not asking God for a religious experience. We are not asking for a spiritual experience. We are asking for a kingdom right to be invoked by the blood of Jesus, one that brings that son or daughter—that citizen—back into alignment with the rights that he or she has because they are a citizen of the kingdom.

WORDS CARRY THE WEIGHT OF THE NATION

Ever notice how, when Jesus spoke, things happened?

***

Jesus: "Lazarus come forth!"
Lazarus: "Whoa! Everybody, I just had the coolest dream!"

***

Jesus: "Peace! Be still!"
Sea of Galilee: "Sorry Jesus. Just having a little fun."

***

Jesus: "OK, fine. Cast the first stone."

Accusers: "We're outta here."

Woman: "Wow!"

***

Jesus governed by his words. When he spoke to people, they were healed, they came to life, they were forgiven. Everything about Jesus brought life to the repentant and conviction to the obstinate.

Let's look at Matthew 8, where Jesus encounters a centurion whose servant was paralyzed.

> *And when Jesus entered Capernaum, a centurion came to Him, begging Him, and saying, "Lord, my servant is lying paralyzed at home, terribly tormented." Jesus said to him, "I will come and heal him." But the centurion replied, "Lord, I am not worthy for You to come under my roof, but just say the word, and my servant will be healed. For I also am a man under authority, with soldiers under me; and I say to this one, 'Go!' and he goes, and to another, 'Come!' and he comes, and to my slave, 'Do this!' and he does it." Now when Jesus heard this, He was amazed and said to those who were following, "Truly I say to you, I have not found such great faith with anyone in Israel. And I say to you that many will come from east and west, and recline at the table with Abraham, Isaac, and Jacob in the Kingdom of Heaven; but the sons of the kingdom will be thrown out into the outer darkness; in that place there will be weeping and gnashing of teeth." And Jesus said to the centurion, "Go; it shall be done for you as you have believed." And the servant was healed at that very moment.*
>
> Matthew 8:5-13

Following the story, we see a centurion who came to Jesus imploring him for healing for his servant. Only, this man had a problem: He was not a citizen of Israel. Still, he was a military leader in charge of a hundred men who, incidentally, were occupying Israel. Clearly, the centurion knew something about authority.

First, he called Jesus "Lord." When you address someone as Lord, you are submitting yourself to them as the person in charge. The word *Lord* means "owner." It's the same as the Hebrew word *adonai*, meaning "owner, one who has authority in a realm, one that owns something, has a right to something."

The centurion said, "Owner, my servant is lying paralyzed at home, fearfully tormented."

Jesus' answer was unequivocal. "I will come and heal him."

Now, just to get the picture, Jesus was not qualifying the centurion. He didn't ask him a series of questions. He didn't say, "You are a Roman. I am not coming to you; I am called to the Jews. It's Jews first, Gentiles second, pal. Especially for you, muscle guy in a leather strap skirt and a brass breastplate."

> *This centurion understood that the Kingdom of God was not a about a quasi-spiritual religious experience. This was about authority conveyed by words, expressing our faith.*

He could have said all of that and still have been within his rights as the Son of God. But he didn't. He said, "I will come."

Why? Because Jesus knew that he could heal the servant if he was in the room with him, mostly likely alone without anybody's unbelief interfering. But notice, when Jesus said, "I will come and heal him," he made a promise. He didn't say, "Let's give this a shot, agree in prayer—you in Latin and I in Aramaic—and we'll see what Father feels like doing today."

That's what religion would do. That's not what Jesus did. He said, "I will come and heal him." Case closed. *Lead the way, Mr. Centurion.*

Yet the Centurion demurred:

"Lord, I am not worthy for you to come under my roof, but just say the word and my servant will be healed. For I am a man under authority, with soldiers under me. And I say to this one, go. And he goes and to another come and he comes, and to my slave, do this and he does it."

When Jesus heard this, he marveled. "Truly, I say to you, I've not found such great faith with anyone in Israel...." We could read it this way: "I've not found such great faith even among covenant people."

This centurion understood that the Kingdom of God was not about a quasi-spiritual religious experience. This was about authority conveyed by words, expressing our faith. "Just give the word, Jesus, and my servant will be good to go." That said it all.

Why was Jesus seeing faith not seen in Israel? Because Jesus was not speaking to a Pharisee or a Sadducee. He was not talking to a temple ruler. He was not speaking with a Jew raised on ancient religious doctrine. He was dealing with a government man who understood authority. The centurion understood what happens when someone with authority—in this case, the owner—speaks an order. Stuff gets done. *Get out of the way, devil.*

3
Culture

When we speak of culture, what do we mean? Let's start with the generally accepted definition.

Culture is the customary beliefs, social forms, and material traits of a racial, religious, or social group.

Merriam-Webster.com Dictionary

We are called to impact the culture of nations. How do we impact them? With our culture—kingdom culture. We are not talking about culture in terms of race, however. We are talking about the *ethnos* of nations.

Ethnos refers to "ethnic group." It has nothing to do with the color of the dirt that God used to form the people. All of us know that dirt comes in different shades. Brown dirt, yellow dirt, pale dirt—it's all dirt. Our *ethnos*—our group; our social form—has many expressions of color. From pale European to the rich obsidian African and every gorgeous shade in between. In the kingdom, however, we don't live life by the color of our dirt.

We are family, all of us. When we live by the color of our dirt, or worse, when we judge others by the color of their dirt, we are living outside the culture of God's kingdom. Racism is ugly and wrong. When we refer to the *ethnos* of nations, we mean a national group of people.

Cultures exist within cultures. There is an American culture—ask any European to describe it for you. (On second thought, maybe not.) Yet within the culture of America are many subcultures...and there are many subcultures to those subcultures, and so on and so forth innumerable.

In our nation of the Kingdom of God, our *ethnos* encompasses only one culture. There is no allowance for subcultures. Why? Because everybody in the Kingdom of God is direct family. There are no cousins in the kingdom. There are no foreigners in the kingdom. Everyone in the kingdom is a son or a daughter. That eliminates subcultures in this capacity. So, when we are looking at one another, we cannot judge each other by any other standards.

Religion tries to do that by asking:

- How much do you pray a day?
- How much do you give every month?
- How often do you read your Bible?
- Do you pray in tongues?
- Do you baptize infants?
- Do your infants pray in tongues?
- Do you read the King James Bible of 1611?
- Does your wife wear makeup?
- Does your husband wear makeup?
- Have you ever watched an R-rated movie?
- Has your dog ever watched an R-rated movie?

Honestly, I could fill the book with these and 8-million other standards of the R.B.I. (Religious Bureau of Investigation). Interesting, though, how the very people who decry the identity politics of the left are the same who...oh, never mind.

Suffice to say that these are examples of the subcultures that religion tries to create. So, in the Kingdom of God, let us eschew such divisive behavior. We are sons or daughters. Certainly, we have unique traits. But these are to highlight God's creative genius. He loves variety. Each of us is unique...just like everyone else!

EQUIPPED FOR SERVICE

We tend to judge others based on material things—wealth, status, standards of living. Just because somebody appears to have more than you have does not make them more important than you. God blesses us with things that pertain to our assignment. As assignments vary, so goes our resources from God.

Somebody told me once, "Greg, you need a jet plane."

"I agree. I need a jet plane."

"Is that a need or a want?" they asked.

"It's a need. I believe that with all my heart. And I believe that a Gulf Stream 650 XL is headed my way one day very soon. Along with the money to maintain it and pay the two pilots that are needed to fly it. Amen. "

"Greg, why do you need that?"

"Because we travel a lot and it would cut out half of our travel time spent waiting in airports. We could do more with that time."

Things that God brings into our lives have to do with our assignments.

Each of us is a different part of the Body of Christ, and different parts require different things to contribute to the function of the whole. So, we cannot look at someone by this world's standard which says, "Well, they have more, so they must be better than I am."

No, they have what their assignment calls for. Someone else might have less. Yet they have all that their assignment calls for. Some of us only need a laptop. Others need a four-wheel drive Jeep to traverse jungle trails. I know people with large houses that are gifted in hospitality. And I know recluses who spend their days isolated in prayer and study; these people are happy with a cardboard box and a box of vanilla wafers.

God is not an equal opportunity king the way the world thinks of equality. He is not interested in everybody getting to the finish line at the same time. We'll each get there on our time...which is God's time. He is a king who distributes his wealth and provision according to assignment and stewardship. As we demonstrate faithfulness with little, he will make us master over much more. Everything in our lives center around assignments—that which God has called us to do.

COMPONENTS OF CULTURE

Culture is composed of a myriad of qualities, among them: material traits, racial traits, religious traits, and social traits. It encompasses the features of everyday existence—the diverse ways of life shared by people in the same place and time. Think of the breakfast table across the globe. In Hawaii, they're eating spam musubi. In the Philippines, it's balut and dried fish. The Germans are feasting on cheese and cold fish. (That explains their sunny dispositions.) In Mississippi, where I'm from, we are defying our cardiologists with buttered grits, fried eggs and ham, and enough coffee to power the Tennessee Valley!

> *God is not an equal opportunity king the way the world thinks of equality.*

The world is a great expression of what it takes for people to exist in different places around the globe. It takes more to do life in Franklin, Tennessee than it does in Tunica, Mississippi, the poorest county in the nation. People in Tunica are doing what they need to get by. They are living, eating, learning, growing and raising families. But the culture has been scaled to a way that they do it differently than people in Franklin, Tennessee. Why?

It costs more to live in Franklin. Groceries, housing, transportation. Things cost even more when we lived in Hawaii. When we left several years ago, a gallon of milk was $10. A loaf of bread was $6.50. It wasn't even the fancy bread with all the little grains on top. This was thin white bread with large holes that the mayonnaise would fall through if you spread it too thick. Life is more expensive in Hawaii. It takes three to five families living in one house just to survive. And that's not a mega-mansion. It could be a 2,000-square-foot house where every family has a bedroom. That is their living area.

Now, you and I cannot think of living like that here. Why? Because we don't have to live like that here. However, other cultures have been drawn into a place to where it is necessary to adapt. Thus, there is a Hawaiian culture, a Franklin culture, and a Tunica, Mississippi culture. There are even cultures within our cultures here of the way people live, provide, grow and do life. There is modern culture and there is good old southern culture. Some cultures are kind of rough. You go into the hood in an inner city somewhere, you can't act like you're from Mayberry, North Carolina. You might die. *Why are you smiling at me? You better take that smile off your face. You have no business smiling at me.*

Attitudes are different. Even within Kingdom University, (a school Joan and I started), there are different cultures and different campuses. Some people call from some of the campuses, and they are just happy to talk to you. They are Joan's best friends on the phone and she has never met them. Others call with an attitude. "Where's my stuff? "Is my stuff coming? I want it now." <CLICK!> It's nothing personal. That's just how they deal with people.

The South has a culture. The North has a culture. The Northeast has an attitude. Within our nation, there are so many different cultures. We as Americans carry an attitude of pride, and it is a healthy pride. You go to Texas and it is a little bit deeper than that. They are proud to be Americans, but they are really proud to be Texans. And even if they move out of Texas, there's still a star hanging on the living room wall and a set of bronzed boots on the doorstep ("Yep. Those were ole' Grand Dad's.) No matter where we go, Joan and I drive around the country and say, "A Texan lives there. We could get help right there if we needed it."

There are all kinds of cultures within America. At our best, however, we are proud to be Americans. We may have differences in our politics and way of life, but when it comes down to being

Americans, we stand as one. We will fight with one another and we will fight for one another. May this stand forever. Glory to God.

ATTITUDES IN THE KINGDOM

In the Kingdom of God, there will be diverse attitudes, but there is one king. It is his attitude that draws everyone together. In a kingdom, unlike a constitutional republic that we have in America, the heart of the king prevails over other hearts. It's not that the hearts of the citizens don't matter. They absolutely matter. The heart of the king unites us all.

> *It's not that the hearts of the citizens don't matter. They absolutely matter. But that the heart of the king unites us all.*

In this kingdom, our dad is the king and everyone in the kingdom is a son or daughter. Ultimately, the king owns everything. Even if his army takes it, it is as if he took it. When a king's army goes out and defeats a city or another nation, the king defeated it.

This is much different than what is taught by religion. Our life in the Kingdom of God is not about our sect of Christianity. No, it is about what the king wants.

In the Bible, the word *Christian* is never used in a positive way. Further, God never refers to believers as Christians. Paul never referred to us directly as a Christians. He only referred to what the pagans were calling us. How does God refer to us in the Bible? He calls us sons and daughters. He calls us citizens, kings, priests and ambassadors…even a peculiar generation (according to the irascible King James).

What does the word *Christianity* literally mean? When most people think about Christianity, they think about the various divisions of Christianity. And why not? What comprises Christianity? We have Roman Catholics, Baptists, Methodists, Presbyterians, Episcopalians, Congregational Churches, Pentecostals, and hundreds of variants of these. We have people who drink, people who abhor drinking, people who dance, people who prance, and people who swear that they are the only ones going to heaven. We even have people whose church services include drinking poison and handling poisonous snakes. They do this in obedience—so they think—to the words of Jesus:

> *These signs will accompany those who have believed: in My name they will cast out demons, they will speak with new tongues; <u>they will pick up serpents, and if they drink any deadly poison, it will not harm them;</u> they will lay hands on the sick, and they will recover.*
>
> Mark 16:17-18

Good thing Jesus included laying hands on the sick, right? Those guys really need that promise. (Oh, and also the promise about raising the dead.)

Is Christianity supposed to be that splintered? Is that how God designed it? No, certainly not. There's to be no division. Yet, if we make Christianity a religion, it will splinter. Why? Because religion organizes itself around doctrine, i.e., belief systems. Believe this way and you're in! *Great! I'm in.* But...don't believe this way and...well, I guess you're out. *Doggone it; now I have to find another church.*

Among Christian denominations, those that manage to stay together the longest are organized around a familial structure. In a word: relationship. This is different than organizing around doctrine. As with any family, your sister is your sister regardless of whether she loads her own ammo and practices taxidermy in the basement, or wears flowers in her hair, moves to California, and roams the streets waving a sign: "Save the Gay Baby Whales for Jesus!"

The kingdom that Jesus came to establish is relationship based. It starts with a relationship with the Father—the "King"—the whole reason for this "dom" in the first place.

When we treat Christianity as a religion, we put it into the same categories as Hinduism, Islam, Buddhism, Taoists and Sikhs.

Remarkably, people who have been in those religions say Christianity's the best one. (Some say it's the only one.)

> *Religion organizes itself around doctrine. Kingdom is relationship based.*

What makes kingdom-focused Christianity different? For starters, we are not in a religious sect. We are part of a nation; it's a country called heaven where we find the Kingdom of God. Further, we worship a king who dwells with us and within us. We don't worship a deity out in the ether. We may have diverse expressions of worship, but there is one focus culminating in a unified expression, and that's the worship of kings to the King.

This is more than just going to church on Sunday, singing a few hymns, a chorus or two of Kumbaya—*"Take the hand of the person next to you"*—and getting some poor sinner saved at the altar. (The same guy who gets saved every week.) That's not a worship service. That's a song service.

Maybe the preacher shares an inspirational message from scripture. But how the word comes to us is very important. Did it come through the correct channels? Is the interpretation correct? Is it truth? Does it follow the rest of the Bible? Scripture in the right hands is dynamite. In the wrong hands, it's still dynamite. It'll just blow you to kingdom come.

THE WALL OF REALITY

The worse aspects of religion have a common source: mankind. The best aspects of the Kingdom of God have the same source. The difference is focus. Lose our focus on the King, and we'll start creating religion before we know it.

Certainly, everything we have done in the past was not wrong. There were many good things to come from the religious denominations. They were doing their best with what they had. I was born-again under that structure. I thank God for the Baptist church.

Culture

It's where I received a call of God on my life. But it couldn't take me much further than that local church. All I had to look forward to from my salvation day was going to heaven. Everything between salvation and heaven was a test, a torture, a trial, something I had to endure to make it to heaven. The goal was to hear God say, "Greg's made it! Come on in, boy!"

Yet when I said the prayer and was baptized, they told me I was automatically saved and going to heaven regardless. So...I'm guaranteed to go to heaven, but I still have to work my tail off to ensure I go to heaven? It was schizophrenic. (What's worse, I didn't even have a tail.)

In any Christian observance, we have to examine the things we do and say to ensure they line up with the Constitution, not of America but of the Kingdom of God. And, if you think that's easy, think again. We need a stable footing before we can even talk about the Kingdom of God. It is a totally different paradigm from what most of us have been raised in. We were taught that we are in a religion called Christianity and the sign of our religion is the cross.

In reality, we are in a government, a kingdom, and the sign of our kingdom is a crown. That is more fitting of the work God has done. We are not Believers because Jesus died on the cross. Nor are we Believers because he rose from the grave. Rather, we are Believers because he was crowned and seated at the right hand of the Father. The cross and the resurrection got him there, but it was the ultimate destination of the crown that makes us who we are today. There can't be a kingdom without a king. We are children of the King. And we are seated with him in heavenly places.

> *...even when we were dead in our wrongdoings, made us alive together with Christ (by grace you have been saved), and raised us up with Him, and seated us with Him in the heavenly places in Christ Jesus*
>
> Ephesians 2:5-6

We could not be seated with him in heavenly places if he had not been seated first.

John 3:3 is the "get into the Kingdom of God" verse—the born-again experience. Jesus is the entryway.

> *Jesus responded and said to him, "Truly, truly, I say to you, unless someone is born-again, he cannot see the kingdom of God."*
>
> John 3:3

> *Jesus said to him, "I am the way, and the truth, and the life; no one comes to the Father except through Me."*
>
> John 14:6

We are Believers because Jesus was crowned and seated at the right hand of the Father.

There is no other way into the Kingdom of God except through Jesus and the born-again experience. The only way to enter the kingdom is through the door. If all we do is stand at the door, we do not experience the interior. All we know of the house is what it looks like from the curb. We are like young men looking for a date.

Many in religious settings accept that truth, but they still keep you at the door. They keep you at the cross. Yet the cross was not the destiny of Jesus. The resurrection and the ascension were his destiny. For in completing that, Holy Spirit could be sent back to us and we could be restored to who he created us to be—his original intent as sons and as daughters.

We cannot intermingle religion and kingdom any more than we can intermingle the world and Christianity. It doesn't fit. It makes a mess of Christianity and the world. So, what in the world do we do? Well, we do what any sane person would do. We come out of our bondage. Not by saying "I am free and all of you people are wrong. Y'all are going to hell," as we point our finger at them.

The truth is most of them are not going to hell. They know Jesus.

Culture

Our responsibility is to say, "Hey, not only have we found the door, but we entered and found some hidden rooms. We have found some places in the Kingdom of God that we were not told of before. Come and experience it with us. Come and live in this beautiful thing called the Kingdom of God and leave behind the religion that has kept you in bondage."

When Jesus returns, that will be the end of one journey but the beginning of another journey, perhaps an eternity of journeys. The finish line will be the starting line. We are on a journey to expand the Kingdom of God, not to expand or to bring any kind of recognition to any form of religion. Where that journey ends—if it ever ends—God only knows.

> *When Jesus returns, that will be the end of one journey but the beginning of another...*

Ever notice how the Bible ends? When Jesus returns? And there's a new heaven and a new earth? All that stuff? Look closely:

And he showed me a river of the water of life, clear as crystal, coming from the throne of God and of the Lamb, in the middle of its street. On either side of the river was the tree of life, bearing twelve kinds of fruit, yielding its fruit every month; and the leaves of the tree were for the healing of the nations.

Revelation 22:1-2

Now let me ask: What is the tree of life for? *The healing of the nations.* Right! It is continually yielding leaves for healing of nations. Now, if everything was done—if our journey was at the end—why is healing still underway? Why do nations still require healing? Clearly, a new journey awaits. We call this promotion. C.S. Lewis phrased it: "Onward and upward."

Kingdom Values, Goals, Practices

Truth

Religion will allow a little truth. The Kingdom provides all truth. We are uncovering truth daily, discovering things that God is revealing, working things out of our lives and working other things into our lives. There are things we need to be doing and things we need to stop doing. We have not arrived, but we are on our way.

Through the influence of Holy Spirit, our lives are promoting a set of values, impacting a generation that is seeking the very things we have from our Father. What are some of the values of the Kingdom of God?

Love

Love is a value. We show the Kingdom of God when we love one another, especially those who persecute us, that say all manner of evil against us! We love them!

> "You have heard that it was said, 'You shall love your neighbor and hate your enemy.' But I say to you, love your enemies and pray for those who persecute you, so that you may prove yourselves to be sons of your Father who is in heaven;"
>
> Matthew 5:43-45

This love that Jesus is talking about has to be experienced before it can be given. It's not a carnal love; it's not transactional. *I give to you so that you give to me.* Rather, it's the love of a perfect father invading your life, causing you to not only be loved but to know that you are worthy of love. See, I can tell you that you are loved, even that I love you, but that only sets up me as the source. However, if I tell you that you are worthy of love—and if you believe me—you open yourself up to love itself. John told us that God is love. So, by accepting that you are worthy of love, you grant God access to your life. No small thing for a life of darkness.

Love has a way of propagating itself. We know we are experiencing true love—the God love—when all we want to do is to love others. Amen? Especially others who are different than we are; others who are predisposed to not like us; others who want to debate and argue with us, as if by putting us down, it will relieve the pressure they feel to admit this light into their beings.

It starts with a smile. Love them and let God do the rest.

Grace

Grace is a value. It's empowerment. It's a right.

Grace is different than mercy. Mercy is when we get what we don't deserve, like getting pulled over for speeding on our way to a meeting and the cop lets us off with a stern warning. Grace is when the cop hands us a hundred-dollar bill for gas money to get us to the meeting.

Morals

Every culture has morals. Without morals, chaos reigns and ultimately, carnage ensues. Survival of the fittest becomes the law of the land.

Many conservative people want certain moral values in our nation, yet all we hear is: You can't legislate morality. Well, yes you can. In fact, people do it all the time.

Marriage is a sacrament between a man and a woman. It is bound by a moral standard. And that distinction is being legislated, for or against, in various places in the country.

Protecting life in the womb is a moral. Again, the culture wars have it both ways, legislating protections and legislating the right to destroy an unborn child. They are legislating morality in that area.

If laws can be enacted to preserve the right to commit immoral acts, then those laws can be replaced with laws to ensure moral acts.

There are many other values that we have in the Kingdom of God that we should express. They have a direct correlation to the manifestation of your attitude. Values will cause attitudes to be expressed.

GOALS OF THE KINGDOM

Every culture has goals. The goal in America, hypothetically, is to create a culture in which everybody can live the American dream. This means equal opportunity amidst an egalitarian culture. Everyone has a chance at a prosperous life. Hard work is rewarded. The means of production remain with the populace, not the government.

> *Grace is a value.*
> *It's empowerment.*
> *It's a right.*

In the Kingdom of God, the goals are not our goals in the sense that they are not for us alone. They must align with the goals of the King. As citizens, our responsibility is to manifest heaven's goals on earth. We are called and equipped to do things in this odd culture called *the world*. As citizens and ambassadors of the kingdom, we are to take the goals of our nation and bring them into this world.

Considering all this, we can conclude that God is clearly interested in this world.

> *For God did not send the Son into the world to judge the world, but so that the world might be saved through Him. The one who believes in Him is not judged; the one who does not believe has been judged already, because he has not believed in the name of the only Son of God. And this is the judgment, that the Light has come into the world, and people loved the darkness rather than the Light; for their deeds were evil.*
>
> John 3:17-19

PRACTICES OF THE KINGDOM

What are the practices of our culture? We don't steal. Right? We don't take the paper clip from our boss' office that he used company money with to buy. We don't take it home and clip our mail together with it. *Well, it is only a paper clip.* Still, what do we call it? Pilfering? Borrowing? IOU? Yeah...you stole it.

Culture

There are many practices in the kingdom, many of which do not align with this present world's culture. In the kingdom, it is illegal to commit adultery. In the world, it is celebrated. (I'm waiting for National Adultery Day.) It is illegal in the kingdom to steal or murder. In the world, some forms of stealing and murder are heralded as rights, the high mark of personal freedom. This is why we are in the world but not of the world. Paul said to the Corinthian church;

> *Or do you not know that the unrighteous will not inherit the kingdom of God? Do not be deceived; neither the sexually immoral, nor idolaters, nor adulterers, nor homosexuals, nor thieves, nor the greedy, nor those habitually drunk, nor verbal abusers, nor swindlers, will inherit the kingdom of God. Such were some of you; but you were washed, but you were sanctified, but you were justified in the name of the Lord Jesus Christ and in the Spirit of our God.*
>
> 1 Corinthians 6:11

The unrighteous will not inherit the Kingdom of God? OK, let's not do those things.

One of the problems we have is trying to bring the world's culture into our kingdom culture, hoping it will work. *It'll be okay. God understands me. I've got a need.* Well, now you are taking away his responsibility to provide for your needs.

To be candid, we all struggle with this. Can a person really work in a sewer all day, come home and not smell like....? None of us do life perfectly. All of us are stiving. Consider Philippians 3:12-14:

> *Not that I have already grasped it all or have already become perfect, but I press on if I may also take hold of that for which I was even taken hold of by Christ Jesus. Brothers and sisters, I do not regard myself as having taken hold of it yet; but one thing I do: forgetting what lies behind and reaching forward to what lies ahead, I press on toward the goal for the prize of the upward call of God in Christ Jesus.*

CHARACTERIZATIONS OF CULTURE

What are the characteristics of this government that God has given us as kingdom citizens? Let's start with the three rules:

1. Everything is made *by* the King.

2. Everything is made *for* the King.

3. Everything belongs *to* the King.

Here's a story of missionaries in Morocco, a kingdom in Africa. One day, the king of Morocco was using the train. These missionaries were at the train station, waiting for hours. Train service was usually timely, but that day they stood all day and, as Americans, grew rather impatient. (Hey, impatience is our national treasure, like hot dogs at a Braves game.)

Venting their frustration to the ticket counter, the missionaries asked where the train was. The Moroccan told them that the king was using the train that day. The missionaries said, "Does the king not know we need to get places? We need the train too."

"You don't understand," answered the Moroccan. "It's the king's train. It's the king's tracks. We get to use them when he's not using them."

That is the way it is in the Kingdom of God. It's God's tracks and God's train. Everything in this nation of heaven belongs to God!

Let's be crystal clear: Everything in the kingdom belongs to God!

Do you remember when Jesus was asked by some Pharisees if it was lawful to pay taxes to Caesar?

> *"Is it permissible to pay a poll-tax to Caesar, or not? Are we to pay, or not pay?"*
>
> *But He, knowing their hypocrisy, said to them, "Why are you testing Me? Bring Me a denarius to look at."*
>
> *And they brought one.*
>
> *And He said to them, "Whose image and inscription is this?"*
>
> *And they said to Him, "Caesar's."*

Culture

And Jesus said to them, "Pay to Caesar the things that are Caesar's, and to God the things that are God's."
And they were utterly amazed at Him.

Mark 12:14-17

Jesus was speaking of ownership. We must give to Caesar what is his and give to God what is his. Whatever bears Caesar's image belongs to Caesar, and whatever bears God's image belongs to God. Pretty simple, eh? It's his property. Of course, Jesus wasn't merely talking about coins. He was talking about ownership. Caesar's image was on the coin. God's image is on you and me and whoever believes in Jesus Christ. Thus, God has ownership rights to us because his image is on us.

When I first discovered that truth, it made me want to run. Why? Because it meant I'm not my own. It's not my image; it's his image on me that gives him an inherent right to me. If I behave outside the bounds of his inherent right (traffic frustrations in Nashville notwithstanding), I am in violation of kingdom culture and law. That is heavy. Why? Because sometimes, I like to get out of the bounds. Sometimes, like a wild basketball, I'll just bounce outside the court without any help. We all do that. But he pulls us back in. I'm glad. Better the King's court than traffic court.

If somebody took your car for a joyride, what would you do? You would call the police! Why? Because they took your property without permission. Well, when you do something God has not authorized, what should God do? You've taken his property without authorization. We've all done that. The beautiful part of conviction is repentance. He's a merciful gracious God for us, but it doesn't give us the right to do what we know is wrong. His mercy is intended to return us to the empowerment of our citizenship rights. Not the rights to operate outside our bounds, but the strength to come back into alignment and operate through grace—the power given us through our king and his kingdom.

Citizenship According to the Kingdom

When we consider the characteristics, institution and organization of the kingdom, we realize that it is about ownership; it is about property. We are part of the property. Every citizen is the property of the nation to which they belong, even Americans. We like to say, "Nobody owns me!" Yet if we dig into our laws, we'll see that we are the property of this nation.

When we join the military, who do we belong to? Uncle Sam. We are not our own anymore. We give up our rights. We surrender our privileges. We sleep when they tell us to sleep. We eat when they tell us to eat. We wear the clothes they tell us to wear. We change our clothes when they tell us to change our clothes. And if we violate any of this, they don't send us home. They send us to the brig, the military jail.

God has ownership rights to us because his image is on us.

As citizens of America, we can lose all of our freedom in a heartbeat. Break a serious rule and we'll be staring at four gray walls. We think we are free...until freedom is stripped from us. Then we realize that it was freedom given us by the nation to which we belong. That same nation can do whatever it will with us.

Kingdom is a serious thing. Religion gives us flexibility. Kingdom brings structure to our lives so we can be prosperous in everything we do. There's only one ultimate agenda: the King's agenda.

Culture and citizenship are very important. There was a day in our nation when people came to America from all over the world, and they assimilated into our culture. They learned to speak English. There was no helpline with "Press 1 for English. Press 2 for Spanish. Press 3 for Sign Language." It was just English. It's still that way in some countries. Germany, for example, gives immigrants two years to pass a German language test and get a job. Failure to do that gets you kicked out. *Jawohl!*

When we come to the Kingdom of God, we don't get to keep our other culture. We have to assimilate. The Kingdom of God has a native

Culture

language; it's heaven's language. It's called tongues. Hallelujah! We need that language to operate in power. It is the king's dialect.

In Kingdom University, we have classes in HGSL—Holy Ghost as Second Language. It is patterned after ESL—English as Second Language. In HGSL, you learn to speak Kingdom. It is to help people in the transition from religion to a place of common kingdom language.

As in all communications, we say things to each other and believe we are being understood, but only until we define the meaning behind our words and expression can we achieve effective communication. This is why we need to know what it *means* to be a son or a daughter, what it *means* to be adopted, what it *means* to be a citizen of the kingdom. (Hey...maybe someone should write a book.)

Christianity is rife with its own terms and phrases that people rarely make the effort to define. Trying to hammer out those definitions can be stressful. People don't like it when their sacred cows are poked. So be it. (I like my steak medium rare.)

My editor, an officious sort, often warns me: "Greg, this is going to upset a lot of people. We might need to change this a bit."

"We can't change it!" I tell him, tossing my cape over my shoulder. "It's got to be this!"

"You're going to upset the applecart," he pleads, practically in tears. "People aren't going to like you anymore!"

"So be it," I declare, face to the sun. "We have to get this right. Somebody's got to put a plow to the ground!"

And so, my editor dutifully writes: "Damn the torpedoes! Full speed ahead!" and the book goes to press.

The concept of adoption, from my book, *Sonship According to the Kingdom*, is a good example of such a sacred cow. Religion teaches that adoption happens when we are born-again. But that's not kingdom adoption; that's not scriptural. I wrote *Sonship* to uncover the truth and broadcast it far and wide.

Adoption is not when we are born-again. It is when we mature and partner with our father in the kingdom business. It's that cultural understanding that comes from asking:

1. Who is speaking?
2. Who are they speaking to?
3. What does it mean in their culture?
4. How do we apply it to our lives?

Damn the torpedoes! Full speed ahead!

From Galatians 4, we know that adoption in the culture Paul was writing to happened when the father brought his son before the community, put his arm around him and held him until no space was between them. The father declared: "Now, today, I adopt my son."

He put a ring on his finger, shoes on his feet, a robe over his shoulders and declared, "When you see him coming, you see me coming. When he shows this ring, he's showing my ring. When you hear him speak, he's speaking for me. When he buys or sells, he's transacting for me."

The son was now fully adopted—a full-grown man. He could be trusted with the father's wealth, the father's land, the father's inheritance, and the father's vision, goals and dreams for the family business. The son was now in a place of maturity where he was not doing things for himself alone, but rather, doing them to promote the prosperity of the family.

Our family business is kingdom business because our daddy is a king! As we mature, we will gradually partner in the family business. It's a matter of trust. The Father knows how far he can trust us. No, not because we are evil, but because we are growing. Galatians 4 tells us that as long as the heir is a child, he is no different from a bondservant. In name, he is the owner of everything. As such, he has an inheritance through his name. He has a father, but he can't be given anything he cannot yet handle. That word *child* in Galatians is the word *orphan*. He's living like a child with an orphan mindset. He's not adopted yet.

Defining our terminology is vital to deeper understanding. Remember, those who control the definitions of a words control the language and the culture.

What do we mean by kingdom? Religion says the Kingdom of God is coming way out in the future. But the Bible tells us in Mark that the Kingdom of God was on the earth within a generation of Jesus walking the earth.

> *And Jesus was saying to them, "Truly I say to you, there are some of those who are standing here who will not taste death until they see the kingdom of God when it has come with power."*
>
> Mark 9:1

> *Defining our terminology is vital to deeper understanding.*

So, we know that the Kingdom of God has come...and it will come! It's a progression. Through our lives and journeys of discovery, we're learning new things that establish the Kingdom of God in a greater way. It is going to be established in a greater way in our world through our sphere of influence.

Now, some of us may experience rejection of the change we offer, indeed, the change we represent. As we bring the Kingdom of God into a place or community, it may seem that they are rejecting us. Well, they're not rejecting us. They're rejecting the king and his kingdom. Why? Usually, it's because religion has a deep hold on their lives. So, what do we do? Just keep hammering away at it until they receive? No. We listen to what Father says. If the father says hammer away, we say, "Send me a bigger hammer, Lord!" If he says buy them a beer, we say "Lite, dark or Pilsner?" If he says to shake the dust off our sandals and walk away, we say "But I'm not wearing sandals, Lord!"

Seriously, it's not about us winning. That's the religious paradigm—the epic battle between good and evil with the souls of mankind as hostages. We raise our 10 lb. King James Bibles above our heads and declare: *I've got to win this thing. I've got to convert them. I've got to bring them in the kingdom. I must save them from hell's eternal flame!*

Yeah...no you don't.

Paul said,

> *I planted, Apollos watered, but God was causing the growth. So then neither the one who plants nor the one who waters is anything, but God who causes the growth.*
>
> 1 Corinthians 3:6-7

So, what is our job? In some cases, we may plant. In other cases, we may water. But either way, God gives the increase. We may get to harvest in fields that we had nothing to do with. If so, we'll do it with joy, singing that great old hymn: "Bringing In the Other Guy's Sheeves!"

When we are obedient to the assignment that Father gives us, our gratification comes from knowing that Father is pleased with our contribution. Let us be content with planting, watering, or reaping, and not become discouraged or disillusioned when we don't see the finished product.

We all play a part in the expansion of the King's influence in a region. They don't always appreciate our contribution. Take comfort in knowing that not everybody you talk to wants to hear your message. You are planting a seed. Someone may want to hear a little bit, and that's all they can handle. On the other hand, if someone says, "Yeah, I'm sick and tired of religion. Show me how me how to get into the Kingdom of God. And do you have any Greg Hood books I could read?"

Guess what? You just reaped where other people planted and watered.

Culture

Forcing the issue by taking someone further than God directs can have a detrimental effect. Let's say we get them into a prayer, and they genuinely give their lives to Jesus. We weep with them. We share our testimony. We pull out pictures of our kids, maybe the ones from our last Caribbean vacation. Then they tell us their story. They show us pictures of their kids being carried away by Child Protective Services.

That's when we look at our watch and exclaim, "Whoa! Where'd the time go?" We slap the new convert on the back and say, "Be ye warmed and filled, Brother. Go and sin no more," as we hop into our Uber and head to our next meeting.

Taking someone further than God directs can have a detrimental effect.

What just happened here? What didn't happen here? There was no discipleship, no follow-up, no responsibility to steward that person. We just opened the guy up like a can of worms, exposed his most vulnerable places in Jesus' name, and blew out of there like the Lone Stranger riding off into the sunset. In a few weeks, days or even hours, that convert will end up worse than he started.

This is why the religious act of holding mass crusades and leading thousands in the sinner's prayer has an upside and a downside. Rejoicing that a hundred thousand people in the Philippines raised their hands at one of our crusades doesn't mean heaven needs to start taking an offering for a new building program. No, we likely had a hundred thousand people say a prayer so that they could get another god in their group of gods, one that might help them get what they want in life. We didn't convert them into the kingdom. We brought them into religion.

That is one reason Joan and I quit doing crusades. There was no follow-up, no discipleship. We gave the names of the converts to all of the spirit-filled churches in the area, but none of those churches followed up. Why? They were operating from a religious perspective, not a kingdom perspective. They didn't want the strain on their resources and facilities.

So, instead of doing crusades, we started building Bible schools to train kingdom-minded apostolic leaders. We installed those leaders in communities before we did an outreach, and we sent new converts to those leaders for follow-up.

CORPORATE CULTURE

It's hard for religion to see the big picture. Religious culture is not corporate. It's individualized. It's about you and your relationship with Jesus—your own personal savior. "Yep, that's him. He lives on top of my dresser. He blesses me every morning, and he's there waiting for me when I get home at night."

Jewish culture was about the culture of the nation, not about individuality.

Religious Christianity is about getting saved and being a good Christian in their church.

Kingdom mentality operates from a corporate culture. Its mindset is the expansion of a single global entity, and that is the Kingdom of God. It is not individualized. It is corporate. It is governmental. It is about the whole. The Kingdom of God is not about keeping your individual relationship with God locked up in your bedroom while you go about your life. It's about your individual relationship with God expanding and joining with others to influence communities, nations, and ultimately the world.

Jewish culture was about the culture of the nation, not about individuality. They understood that the actions of one person affected the whole nation.

Religion it is not like that. In religion, if you backslide, leave or stray, it doesn't affect anybody but you. But in the kingdom, when you mess up, it affects all of us. It was the same in Jewish history. This is why individual sin was dealt with so harshly. "It ain't just about you, Hezikhakkalam. You're gonna get us all killed."

Recall in Joshua 7, when Israel fought against Ai, that little town on the hill. It didn't go so well. Israel had just defeated the mighty city of Jericho and now were up against this punk town that could only afford two letters in its name. Israel lost…badly.

Joshua fell on his face, wondering how they had lost this battle. How did their nation lose to this insignificant foe?

Turns out one guy, Achan, had hid some stuff beneath his tent—stuff that God said to destroy after they defeated Jericho. His sin affected the entire nation, and that's why they lost to Ai. The repercussions were dire. He and his whole family were destroyed. God wiped out their lineage.

Folks, this is the kingdom. Kingdom needs us in position, doing our job with integrity in this governmental structure. It's about fulfilling the will of the Father and expanding his kingdom into the earth. If one of us fails, we all fail. If one succeeds, we all succeed. If one hurts, we all hurt. If one rejoices, we all rejoice. It's about us collectively!

> *And if one part of the body suffers, all the parts suffer with it; if a part is honored, all the parts rejoice with it.*
>
> 1 Corinthians 12:26

Paul refers to us as being part of a body.

> *For the body is not one part, but many. If the foot says, "Because I am not a hand, I am not a part of the body," it is not for this reason any less a part of the body. And if the ear says, "Because I am not an eye, I am not a part of the body," it is not for this reason any less a part of the body. If the whole body were an eye, where would the hearing be? If the whole body were hearing, where would the sense of smell be? But now God has arranged the parts, each one of them in the body, just as He desired. If they were all one part, where would the body be? But now there are many parts,*

but one body. And the eye cannot say to the hand, "I have no need of you"; or again, the head to the feet, "I have no need of you."

1 Corinthians 12:14-21

Ours is a corporate culture comprised of particular members. It takes all of us to be able to do what the Body of Christ is supposed to do. This corporate group is the ekklesia.

> *If one fails,*
> *we all fail.*
> *If one succeeds,*
> *we all succeed.*
> *If one hurts,*
> *we all hurt.*
> *If one rejoices,*
> *we all rejoice.*

What they are doing in Winslow, Arizona (presumedly while standing on a corner) affects what we are doing in Franklin, Tennessee. What they are doing at nine o-clock in Boise, Idaho affects what others are doing in Missouri. What they do in the Philippines affects the Washington, D.C. area. I'm not sure anything affects California...but we're praying anyway!

Our strength comes from the corporate anointing, not merely the individual anointing. Jacquie Tyre wrote, *The Corporate Armor*, a powerful teaching of how the ekklesia works corporately to accomplish the task of kingdom expansion. We are all in this together.

IMPARTING CULTURE

In business, corporate cultures focus on the bottom line; but they get there through a set of common values, convictions, and social practices associated with a particular field or activity. The integrated pattern comes from the aggregate of human knowledge, beliefs, and behavior that depends upon the capacity for learning and transmitting knowledge to succeeding generations. To be integrated means "to blend, to unify the whole, to unite, to incorporate." The integrated pattern of human knowledge, belief and behaviors depends upon the capacity for learning. Yet not only learning but also transmitting. Not just taking in, but also being able to give out. Transmitting knowledge to succeeding generations transfers culture.

Culture is generational. There are things I do or see in my life that remind me of my dad. (Man, he was a handsome fellow!) I see both my parents in the way I laugh, talk and react to situations. My family's culture was passed down to them, and they passed it down to me and my brother. I learned it without even trying. Culture was imparted through influence as I learned to imitate my family. The same holds true in the kingdom. Paul told us:

Be imitators of me, just as I also am of Christ.

1 Corinthians 11:1

Paul was saying, "Do what I'm doing. As I'm doing what Christ did, you do what I did." He was imparting a culture by transmitting the culture he received from Christ. The most substantial growth is generational. It is transmitting along family lines, not verbal so much as demonstrated. Children don't learn from what we say but from what we do. Funny thing is, we are always doing something, so we are always imparting something. Might as well make it good things.

Culture is contagious. My family worked at creating a peaceful environment for my brother and me to grow up in. We had provision and were safe. That culture was transmitted to me, and I transmitted that to my children. Joan and I have that culture in our home. What her parents gave her joined with what my parents gave me.

As much as culture is absorbed, we still must be intentional about it. What example are we setting? Do we really think we can hide this act or disguise this trait?

America has always been a nation of pioneers. God is using this nation today to teach future generations that they don't have to live in religion. There is another kingdom and culture called the Kingdom of God.

Culture is enlightenment. It is an excellence of taste acquired by experience. It cultivates a refined desire, elevating what we prefer and expect. My wife, Joan, has expensive taste. That's why she married me. She's the daughter of the king. She wants kingly things. And so she should. She would rather have an original purse than a knockoff, even though both hold her things just fine. It's a matter of authenticity.

Culture creates the appreciation of finer taste. Who we associate with determines our taste. If we hang around deep country folk in overalls and tank tops, we'll cultivate a taste for fried baloney, Skoal, country music and NASCAR. But if we hang around writers and editors who love filet mignon and expensive French Bordeaux, we're going to run up quite a bill at Outback.

This is why we must be careful who we join with. Some impartations are good; others are not so good. What did Paul tell us in Romans?

> *The most substantial growth is generational.*

And do not be conformed to this world, but be transformed by the renewing of your mind, so that you may prove what the will of God is, that which is good and acceptable and perfect.

Romans 12:2

The first thing to be influenced is usually not our minds. It's our hearts. We'll find ourselves moved by an influence, and our intellect comes along to justify it for us. The subconscious part of our being stores the patterns, habits and experiences. We absorb and transmit culture without even thinking. It's like stepping into a shower and getting soaked.

Paul was identifying the process of renewing our hearts and minds. Our hearts must be directed to God in everything we do. Our subconscious being must be influenced through an acquired, enlightened taste. My taste is no longer for religion. My taste is for kingdom. I don't want to wear those religious garments anymore. I want to wear the garments of praise, worship and corporate anointing. I don't want to sing songs. I want to enter into the Holy of Holies. I don't want rituals and rules. I want blessings and life.

This is a transformation, though one we cannot merely claim consciously. It requires a retraining of our hearts and minds. It requires new experiences to replace old ones. If we were battered in one situation, the same situation will come around again, only this time, we'll be guided by Holy Spirit. "Hey Greg, remember that bully who used to push you around? Here he comes again. Oh, and Greg? Today's the day, Boy."

We absorb things subconsciously all the time. Madison Avenue knows this. We don't have to be told: "Buy these slacks." Instead, we are shown a picture of a sleek, sophisticated beauty gliding down the aisle in said attire, and our inner voice says, "I want those!" (Right before our wife smacks us upside the head.)

Paul's words to the Romans conveyed action. "Don't be conformed...be transformed...renew your mind." Why? "That you may prove...live out...the good, acceptable, and perfect will of God."

It's a *do*, not a *done to us*.

I've heard people preach the three wills of God: the good, the acceptable, and the perfect. Well, that teaching is neither good, acceptable nor perfect. It's garbage. There's one will of God; it is good, acceptable, and perfect.

Everything about Paul's message to the Romans was rooted in intentionality. The Romans were doers. They built cities, innovated water distribution with aqueducts, installed sanitation. Oh...and in their spare time, they conquered most of the known world. These were not guys who sat around at night waiting for the final tally on Rome's Got Talent.

Listen to the force behind Paul's words at the beginning of chapter 12:

Therefore, I urge you, brothers and sisters, by the mercies of God, to present your bodies as a living and holy sacrifice, acceptable to God, which is your spiritual service of worship.

Romans 12:1

"I urge you...present yourselves...a living sacrifice." In writing, we call this the active voice. I can hear Paul's emphasis, made more remarkable by the realities of the day. Writing was difficult in Bible times. Pens came from pigeons, ink from octopuses, and parchment was once the backside of a sheep. People didn't mince words in those days. They couldn't afford to. (I'm sure the sheep appreciated that.)

> *There's one will of God; it is good, acceptable and perfect.*

Paul was speaking to his new converts through his apostolic grace. He had a lot to say.

I say to everyone among you not to think more highly of himself than he ought to think; but to think so as to have sound judgment, as God has allotted to each a measure of faith.

Romans 12:3

Religion says you should not think highly of yourself. But this scripture does not say that. It says you should not think *more* highly of yourself than you should. You should think highly of yourself, but not more highly. What's the difference? If you are good at something, own it. I'm good at some things, great at others, and a dismal failure at other things. In all things, however, I am a work in progress. Another day to be alive, to grow! Glory to God!

Paul is telling us that the way we live, present ourselves to others, and relate to God is determined by how well we renew our mind. Not just whether we love God or not. That is consciously in front of us. I know I love him. Renewal goes deeper. It affects the patterns we've learned subconsciously, those rooted in the heart, inhabiting the subconscious mind, informing our intellect. It affects our decisions, steers our life, dictates what we do, what we believe, how we act, how we react, how we present things and how we receive things. It is the belief system within us that we are living out.

A friend once told me: The most important choices we make in life are related to who and what we admit into our lives. To admit is closely related to another word: *believe.*

The verb *believe* is mentioned over 200 times in the New Testament. There's a reason for this. Jesus came not to restore a religion, but to reclaim his people—the human race. To do so requires a transformation, and that requires a change in our belief structure. "If you believe…."

> *The most important choices we make in life are related to who and what we admit into our lives.*

Paul was telling the Roman church, who were living like Romans and trying to be mature, that they can't be like rampaging conquering invaders. They needed to change the way they thought and how they conducted themselves toward God and man. It's the same principle undergirding John the Baptist's message to the Jews, although he just said it a bit more succinctly.

Repent, for the kingdom of heaven is at hand.

Matthew 3:2

Paul was speaking to a foreign nation and chose his language accordingly. John was speaking to the home crowd. He knew his people. So, he didn't have to explain as much. We understand his message as: "Change the way that you are thinking so you can change the way you conduct your life. It will change how you perceive things. It will change how you give things and react to things. All of these things are in your subconscious mind, and that dictates how you do life."

Indeed, this is what kingdom culture is all about. Immersion brings enlightenment. It creates an excellence of taste, a kingdom taste. It's acquired by an intellectual training and subconscious exposure. It's unlearning and learning. It's cultivating living materials in a prepared media—a culture that grows within us.

1 Corinthians 5:6 says, "A little leaven leavens the whole lump." This works for good lumps and bad lumps. The kingdom culture that you and I carry invades a living place where it can grow and bring life to a place that never had life.

We are taking the Kingdom of God into new environments—places that need it. We are leavening them. We carry within us the nutrition to nurture life in an unnatural environment. It's leaven, and just a little bit leavens the whole batch. This is the power of our culture.

Our culture is contagious. It's infectious. When it gets on people, they can't help but break free of sin. We see this happening in congregations, in schools, in businesses. People receive our culture because it answers a longing; it feeds a hunger; it uncovers a strong desire they do not have words to express. It is the kingdom they are longing for, but they find themselves in environments where kingdom does not naturally grow. It's been eradicated. Until we come along.

Boom!

Kingdom culture is growing. People are catching it. Families are catching it. It's reaching dead religious places and bringing them to life. Nothing can stop it. Kingdom is breaking out everywhere. In our workplaces, our families, everywhere we go, we are the leaven—the leaven of heaven. Hallelujah. We carry the kingdom everywhere we go.

Cultivation develops intellectual and moral facilities, especially by education or retraining. That is why it's important to learn, not to memorize but to learn. There's a difference between memorizing scripture and learning scripture.

The two kingdoms that operate today are the Kingdom of Light and the Kingdom of Darkness. The Greek word for *darkness* means,

Culture

"ignorance." It doesn't mean "an evil, dark, demonic shroud with diabolical power." The Kingdom of Darkness is a kingdom of ignorance. The power that the enemy has in the lives of humans is facilitated through ignorance.

My people are destroyed for lack of knowledge.
Since you have rejected knowledge

Hosea 4:6

Clearly, ignorance is a dark and evil thing. On the other hand, the word *light*, as in Kingdom of Light means, "knowledge."

Now concerning spiritual gifts, brethren, I would not have you ignorant.

1 Corinthians 12:1 KJV

Notice that in both kingdoms, the definitions are vastly different from how religion defines them.

Religion defines *darkness* as that evil, dark cloud coming into your life and tormenting you. It also defines *light* as this illumination of Jesus that draws people to him. Think of the starlight radiating above the manger in Jerusalem. But these descriptions are paltry and ineffective. They are beyond our reach, impervious to our influence. When we understand that darkness is ignorance and light is knowledge, we know what to do.

Kingdom knowledge creates kingdom culture. We acquire culture through learning, experience and discipline. It's intentional. In kingdom culture, we have to be intentional about everything we do. We are developing intellectual and moral facilities through education, by demonstration in everything we do. That is our kingdom culture.

This is why the study of citizenship, sonship and kingdom requires us to be very intentional to educate ourselves. Still, knowledge alone is not enough. Holy Spirit takes that knowledge and converts it into power. That power is the cultural change we need in everyday life. Knowledge without Holy Spirit can easily devolve into memorization and mindless allegiance. When we truly learn something, we practice it. It becomes a part of us. We no longer have to think; it's automatic. This is how we implement the kingdom in everyday life. It's not just something we learn and regurgitate. It has to be practical, able to be put in practice, to be walked out and demonstrated. It's how we do life.

THE SOUND OF THE NATION

Music is a powerful tool for imparting learning and experience. People get much of their knowledge from the music they sing. King David knew this well. This is why we revere the Psalms. Unfortunately, most of the music in churches is full of weak and inaccurate theology.

> *Kingdom knowledge creates kingdom culture.*

Let us be mindful of the power of music and choose what we will admit into our lives. There are songs I refuse to sing. I'm just not going to do it. Further, I'm not going to allow them to be sung in places where I am leading.

Yet this effort is not simply a matter of censorship. We need to educate our songwriters. Many have come out of a culture of depression, poverty, shattered homes and hopelessness. When we walk in the Kingdom of God, we discover that the answer to all those things is wrapped up in one person: Jesus.

> *And the church is his body; it is made full and complete by Christ, who fills all things everywhere with himself.*
>
> Ephesians 1:23 NLT

All things are summed up in Christ Jesus. *All things.* Jesus said he didn't come to do away with the law and the prophets, he came to fulfill those things.

> *Think not that I am come to destroy the law, or the prophets: I am not come to destroy, but to fulfil.*
>
> Matthew 5:17 KJV

Culture

Jesus fulfilled everything. He is the fullness of everything. All we need is in our king...and some new songs!

I suspect that one reason God started Kingdom University in Franklin, Tennessee, is because of its proximity to Nashville, where much of America's music comes from. Many of the nation's musicians, entertainers and studios are in this area. God wants to influence the sound of the nation through the songs of the nation. This affects the belief structure of a nation.

We can follow the songs throughout history and understand the broader history of those places and times that birthed them.

For example:

When we all get to Heaven
what a day of rejoicing that will be.

I hate that song. Why? Because it says I have to wait to get to heaven before I can rejoice. That's terrible theology. We can rejoice now. We should rejoice now. Oh, it's a catchy tune but the theology is rotting garbage on a humid August morning.

Here's another:

I'll fly away old glory.
I'll fly away.
When I die
Hallelujah bye and bye
I'll fly away.

Really? No, I am not looking to fly away. I am ruling and reigning with God right here, right now. We don't go to heaven. We get a new earth, hopefully a better earth, and we set up shop there. We ain't flying nowhere!

Yet these songs are powerful. This is why the weight of God is on the music community to produce music in line with truth. Sure, some truth is how we're feeling today. Saying "You done stole my heart and squashed that sucker flat," is a good start, but it's not the end. God's deliverance, healing and restoration is the end of all suffering. Let's write that into the final verse! We are seeing new songs, new sounds being birth out of this region, music that ushers in the kingdom.

The old joke goes like this:

Q. What do you get when you play a country song backwards?

A. Well...your wife takes you back, your dog comes home, you sober up and the bank man gives you back your truck.

We need to reverse the songs our society fawns over.

I once gave a word to a young man in Chattanooga. Part of that word was that he was going to write non-Christian songs. Further, he was going to find himself sitting with people and writing songs, not over a cup of coffee or some herbal tea but over a beer.

Now, that messes with religion big time. But the Lord said that young man is going to help shift the music industry.

> *We need to reverse the songs our society fawns over.*

Growing up, I wanted to be a Country music star. That was my goal in life. It is in my veins. My dad was a traveling musician. You can find him in the Rockabilly Hall of Fame. As a young man, I had a band and we won talent shows all over the country. We won a recording contract. We won a van. We won a scholarship to the Philadelphia Theatrical Academy of Arts. We played for senators. We even played for President Ronald Reagan in the rotunda of the White House. And when we got our biggest booking, our band broke up. It was busted flat in Baton Rouge; down to seeds and stems once again; gone, gone...the damage done. All that.

I never got to do the things I'd dreamed of. Why? I wanted to be part of the music industry I'd grown up with, but my pursuit of it was taking me further from God's calling. I was called for something else, something more for me. So, God cut off the music part of me. It wasn't until 40 years later that I developed an influence with some key people in the music industry.

When I ask the Lord: *Why did you bust up the band?* I knew the answer immediately. It was so I wouldn't become absorbed by the music industry. Today, I can bring solutions to it; I can bring the Kingdom of God. And for that, I am eternally grateful.

Culture is very important. God had to develop a kingdom culture in me before he could lead me to the place that he wanted me to influence.

It's the same with you. There are places where God wants you to have influence. Big places, little places, hidden places, obscure places. He wants to bring you before people who have influence: kings, presidents, people who steer nations. God wants to do that with you, but he has to mature you in kingdom before he can put you in those environments. He had to get the religion out of me and get the kingdom into me. He'll do the same for all of us.

4

Ambassador

Ambassador: An official envoy, a diplomatic agent of the highest-rank accredited to a foreign government or sovereign as the resident representative of his or her own government or sovereign or appointed for a special and often temporary diplomatic assignment.

Merriam-Webster.com Dictionary

THE WORLD'S EUPHEMISMS for our existence abound.

- Here today, gone tomorrow.
- We're food for worms, lads.
- Life stinks, then you die.
- There's no such thing as gravity; the earth sucks.

Despite these and many other dark and pessimistic sayings, the fact remains that we are only temporary on this earth…at least this time around. The Bible reminds us every chance it gets.

> *…it is destined for people to die once, and after this comes judgment,*
>
> Hebrews 9:27

> *Yet you do not know what your life will be like tomorrow. For you are just a vapor that appears for a little while, and then vanishes away.*
>
> James 4:14

Citizenship According to the Kingdom

Our term here on Terra Firma will end one day, unless the Lord returns first. What, then, shall we do with this marvelous experience called *living*? Ah, the universal question. We grow up, meet someone, fall in love, raise our kids, keep a small garden out back, be a friend to our neighbors, get regular checkups and wait for the day when we hear: "You're a very sick man, Mr. Smith. The slightest shock...could kill you." THUD!

There must be something more. Fortunately, there is. We are diplomatic agents for the Kingdom of God.

> *Therefore, we are ambassadors for Christ, as though God were making an appeal through us; we beg you on behalf of Christ, be reconciled to God.*
>
> 2 Corinthians 5:20

Paul uses the term *ambassadors* to address believers in Christ. Like all things kingdom, this is a governmental title, not a religious title. Paul understood the governmental nature of Christianity despite being a member of the F.P.I., (Former Pharisees of Israel), the most extreme religious cult of his day. When Romans looked up *religion* in the dictionary, there was a picture of Paul beating some poor Christian with a scroll.

By definition, an ambassador is a diplomatic agent of high rank. The highest diplomat we have in our nation is the Secretary of State. He or she is the diplomat of diplomats, the ambassador of ambassadors. They have charge over embassies all over the world and exercise tremendous influence over foreign relations.

Jesus functioned the same way. In modern terminology, Jesus was the Secretary of State. He returned to the earth to reestablish heaven's embassy. He took back what the first Adam had given away. Adam was the Chief Ambassador in this colony known as earth. God created earth as an extension of heaven. He wanted to expand his kingdom. He set Adam in the earth as an ambassador. God gave him dominion and set him in as a king. Unfortunately, Adam gave up his kingship to a knave.

When Jesus returned to take back what the first Adam squandered, he established ambassadors from the home country, starting with his 12 disciples. Paul carried through with this analogy, explaining that we are ambassadors, representatives of a government, not dour devotees of a dark religious order. We are diplomatic agents of high rank. We represent the Kingdom of God.

Our position on the earth is not that of a lowly sinner saved by grace. We are not trying to survive earth so we can crawl into heaven. We are sons and daughters who carry diplomatic ranking from the kingdom we are from, not the nation we live in. Glory!

> *We are sons and daughters who carry diplomatic ranking from the kingdom…*

As we go through our daily lives, we carry diplomatic rank 24/7, 365 days a year. Isn't that amazing? That changes everything. We are not church members; we are diplomats. And every diplomat embodies the qualities of the nation that they are from. They do not represent the nation that they are in.

We embody the Kingdom of God, not the systems of this world. Ours is the governmental structure of heaven. That is hugely different than what religion teaches.

LEGAL ISSUES

In Christianity today, we have been taught to approach legal issues from a religious standpoint. Here is the fact: Everything we do has spiritual ramifications. Everything we experience touches the unseen realm. From the moment we lie down to when we lie down the next night and everything in between, we are in contact with the spirit as well as the natural. Why? Because we are part spirit just as our creator is spirit.

> *God is spirit, and those who worship Him must worship in spirit and truth.*
>
> John 4:24

So, when seeking our provision as citizens of the kingdom, we are not looking for God to do something spiritual. We already are spiritual. The real divide is whether we are looking for a religious manifestation or a governmental manifestation. Religion tries to find ways to please God so he'll do what we ask. Governmental knows where we stand in God, and it asserts its God-given rights.

This is how Jesus walked with God. He did not walk as a religious man, even though he adhered to Jewish customs. He went to the temple. He paid taxes. He read from scripture on the sabbath in his hometown. (That last time nearly got him killed.) He did all those things because he was born into the Jewish culture. But Jesus operated as a government representative from the Kingdom of God. He dealt with the root causes of people's maladies. His words contained the authority of the owner, and as such, they conveyed the power of the creator to make things right.

Our words are powerful. As citizens of the Kingdom of God, our words carry the weight of the nation. Why? Because we are not simply citizens. We are ambassadors.

> *Therefore, we are ambassadors for Christ, as though God were making an appeal through us; we beg you on behalf of Christ, be reconciled to God.*
>
> 2 Corinthians 5:20

As citizens of the kingdom, we embody the government of heaven in our lives. We carry it everywhere we go. We are citizens who owe allegiance to our heavenly government and are entitled to protection and provision from it.

An ambassador is the embodiment of a nation in a foreign land. An ambassador doesn't have to worry about his or her immediate needs.

Consider a politician who runs for office. They still have to pay their mortgage and utility bills. They still need to buy food and care for everything in their life when they campaign for political office. A politician even has to also ask for the position. "I'm seeking this office.

Ambassador

I am filling out my papers. I'm getting the signatures I need. I'm putting up signs. I'm campaigning. I am running for Senate. I'm hiring a lawyer. I deny everything. I'm asking you to vote for me so I can get into this position of authority."

Jesus' words contained the authority of the owner; they conveyed the power of the creator to make things right.

An ambassador is different. Ambassadors never run for office. They are simply appointed. They receive a phone call one day from someone in the State Department: "Hey, Billy Bob, I need you to represent America in Brazil. That's right. Load up yer truck, boy. They're waiting on you down at the embassy."

When ambassadorship is conferred upon them and they relocate to Brazil (or wherever), they don't pay a mortgage. They don't pay utilities, food, taxes, or a car loan. Even their gas is provided. Why? Because America provides those things for them as an ambassador in a foreign land.

Now, as Born-again Believers—as citizens of the kingdom—we should ask ourselves: where do we live? We are *in* this world, but we are not *of* this world. We are ambassadors of God's kingdom. Glory to God! Our provision as ambassadors is realized when we go home and declare that all we have: the land, the house, the boat, the outbuildings, and a motorcycle or two, God has given us as an embassy. Hallelujah!

"God, this is your embassy. Your ambassador lives here. Thank you, Lord, for all the provisions that we need. May we spread your influence to the ends of the earth. Or at least, the driveway. Glory!"

This understanding shifts everything. No longer am I focused on trying to feed my family or pay our bills. Oh...they still get paid. The difference is, God is helping me. He does those things in creative ways. Maybe he gives me a job and some influence for a promotion. Maybe he gives me a place to invest and provides an income stream. Maybe I learn to apply his authority to getting my spending in order. The key is that everything I do now is through my ambassadorship. I am living on earth to influence the nations—the *ethnos* that are around me—with the Kingdom of God. My assignment is not to make a living. My assignment is to expand the Kingdom of God.

So, whatever we are doing—a job, a career, in school, raising kids, developing businesses—our core assignment is kingdom expansion. Sure, we will earn an income through the economy, but with the lifestyle of the assignment God has given us, that income alone is not going to be enough. Our assignment is always going to be bigger than our paycheck. It is always going to be that way. God loves to stretch us. That is how we grow.

If our assignment is not bigger than our income, one or two things are going to happen. God is going to either increase our assignment or shrink our income. Why? So he can get the glory. So he can be the king in our lives. This may sound contrary, even mean-spirited, but it's not. This is how he leads us to greater resources than we could ever get on our own.

Jesus governed by his words. Kings govern by their words. Ambassadors govern by their words. They speak on behalf of the state or the nation they represent.

When I am in another nation, my citizenship doesn't change. I don't have to get citizenship in the Philippines every time I visit there. I remain an American. My citizenship is not based on where I am. It is based on where I am from, and that determines what I represent.

We cannot be an ambassador without being a citizen. God has placed us here, even though we are no longer from here. Our citizenship doesn't change just because we live and work in this world. This worldly system does not gauge how we live, how we function or who takes care of us. The world is not something God is trying to destroy. He is trying to restore and redeem it according to John 3:17 and 19.

Ambassador

For God did not send the Son into the world to judge the world, but so that the world might be saved through Him.

And this is the judgment, that the Light has come into the world.

Jesus was not sent here to judge the world but to restore it. You and I are in this earth as kingdom citizens, as ambassadors, to restore and redeem the world through Jesus Christ.

FOREIGN EMBASSIES

> *Jesus governed by his words. Kings govern by their words*

I have had the privilege of being in several embassies throughout the world. One of those embassies was in Guyana, one of the poorest countries on earth. I think that is where they manufacture and distribute mosquitoes, because them buggers are big down there.

Poverty is endemic throughout Guyana. During our visit, our associate pastor, Steve, and I were sharing a room in a Guyana hotel. I decided to take a shower before dinner. I turned the water knob and all I heard was groaning and rattling as the water tried to make its way through the pipes. Pipes rattled in the floor and the walls. The faucet was wide open, but nothing was coming out. Finally, it began spitting all kinds of nasty gross stuff into the tub. I stared at the viscous pool forming around my feet. *What do I do?* I cleaned it up and let the muck run until it became a semi-clear stream of fluid.

That experience was foreign to me. It was a part of the nation I was visiting, not the nation I belonged to. In America, we would have called the health department and set up a quarantine for half a city block.

While in Guyana, I visited the US embassy. Walking in was like entering the Ritz Carlton in New York City. Fine marble floors, mahogany wood, modern conveniences like water fountains that didn't kill you and toilets that actually flushed without pouring water into them. Even the food was excellent, better than anything I ever had in America.

Although I was in Guyana, when I stepped into that embassy, I stepped into the United States of America. When I walked out of that embassy, I was back in another nation. But while inside that embassy, I was in the United States of America. It was the government property of the United States of America. It did not belong to the host nation.

As believers—as citizens of the kingdom—we are ambassadors in this world, representing the nation we hail from—heaven. We no longer belong to the nation we presently occupy. We are ambassadors of the Kingdom of God, not the First Church of Pass the Plate in Peoria, Illinois. (No offense intended to the fine folks of Peoria.)

The US ambassador in Guyana can step out of the embassy, walk the streets of Guyana, go to different places and do anything he wants in Guyana. He can visit the poorest areas or meet with the President of Guyana in his palace. No matter where he goes, his citizenship never changes because he carries the nation of the United States with him.

This is why we, as God's citizens and ambassadors, we are not simply trying to survive this world. As ambassadors of heaven, we carry the government of heaven everywhere we go. We have everything that our nation has to offer. We embody our country. We speak for our country. We are not only in our country; our country is in us.

As Jesus said:

> *"The kingdom of God is not coming with signs that can be observed; nor will they say, 'Look, here it is!' or, 'There it is!' For behold, the kingdom of God is in your midst."*
>
> Luke 17:20-21

THY WILL

Ambassadors speak for their nations, but they don't speak their own will. They speak the will of the head of state. Therein lies the power of an ambassador. Why? Because when you speak your own will, you are no longer acting as an ambassador. If you start expressing your opinions as policy and make your own decisions for the nation you represent, you will be recalled by that nation. And when you get recalled, you are out of a job.

In the Kingdom of God, when you get recalled, you don't get to walk on the earth anymore. You go back to the home country, which is heaven. As ambassadors, we cannot speak on our own will. We don't have that right; we don't have the privilege to speak on our own. Everything we say and do must be aligned with our head of state—our Father.

Throughout this journey, this assignment of life on earth, we are to constantly ask the Father:

- What do you say about this?
- What is your position on this?
- What do I need to address?
- What do I need to bind?
- What do I need to loose?
- What do I need to curse?
- What do I need to bless?

An ambassador's focus is not on his comfort or ease, where he'll eat or sleep, or how he'll keep the lights on. That is the responsibility of the sponsoring nation. An ambassador's focus is on representing the will of the home country and keeping its leaders informed.

Let this understanding transform you. We are not sinners trying to make it to heaven the best we can. We are sons and daughters, ambassadors of our home country of heaven. And we have the entire nation backing us in the assignments God has given us as we operate in the influence he has given us. We are here to enlarge the interests of heaven.

Religion doesn't teach that. Religion does not give us that privilege. It cannot. But kingdom can...and does.

CONSTITUTIONAL COVENANT

The power of citizenship is found in a constitutional covenant. Our citizenship in America is only as good as our constitution. Anytime people form a government, they create a constitution. It consists of rules, laws, and rights that are brought together to set up the structure of how that nation functions. In the United States, students are taught civics. We learn about the Constitution, its amendments, including the Bill of rights (the first 10 amendments), and the government structure it mandates. By this, we understand our position as citizens of the United States.

As Born-again Believers, we are also governed by a constitutional covenant. What is our constitution? The Bible. It delineates our rights, privileges, and responsibilities as citizens. Everything the king of our nation said that he would do to ensure our protection and our provision is wrapped up in that holy book. It is a constitution of sorts. In the past, we may have looked at the Bible as a religious book. Yet as we examine the chapters, sub-chapters and subpoints, we realize we can refer to these things as legal standing, not wishful thinking.

> *We are spirit, soul and body. And our body is what makes us legal in this world.*

For example, we don't have to stand before God and ask: "Father, would you please heal me?"

We don't have to ask for that which is already ours. We claim it by decreeing it with our words. Our mouth—the portal of our speech—is the most important part of our being. We are spirit, soul and body. And our body is what makes us legal in this world. (More on this in chapter 7.)

Covenant in scripture was sealed by blood. As Born-again Believers, the blood of Jesus sealed our covenant. This is the blood covenant we have with Christ. Through it, we have citizenship—the rights, privileges, provisions and responsibilities of being a citizen of the Kingdom of God.

Jesus did not come to establish a religion. He came to birth and build a church, an ekklesia, a government. The mission of Jesus is to restore the earth to his territory. Remember, all kingdoms have territory that determines their wealth and their standing.

> *The earth is the Lord's, and the fullness thereof;*
> *the world, and they that dwell therein.*
>
> Psalm 24:1 KJV

All the governing systems and structures in this world are coming under subjection to the Kingdom of God because we, his people, are in this world.

> *Then the seventh angel sounded; and there were loud voices in heaven, saying,*
>
> *"The kingdom of the world has become the kingdom of our Lord and of His Christ; and He will reign forever and ever."*
>
> Revelation 11:15

This scripture tells us that our responsibility is to cause the kingdoms of this world to become the Kingdom of our God. The governments of this world are becoming the governments of our God. Glory!

RESTORATION

Jesus came to earth to restore the Kingdom of God on earth. He came to restore to earth the government of God.

Note: people often make note of the difference between the Kingdom of Heaven and the Kingdom of God. In fact, they are one and the same. Matthew used Kingdom of Heaven instead of Kingdom of God because he was writing to Jews, and they felt that to even say "God" was blasphemous.

Citizenship According to the Kingdom

For our purposes, I might refer to the fact that the Kingdom of God is the influence of heaven in a territory. When I mention heaven, I'm referring to it as a place where God's kingdom originates. The Kingdom of God is in heaven, but it is not yet fully on earth.

Almost every county in the nation has a federal building. That is where court takes place. That is where the U.S. Marshals are. That is a federally run facility. So, the Supreme Court, the Congress, the Executive Branch are in D.C.; and that would be a picture of the Kingdom of God in heaven where everything federally is run from the nation. Your federal outpost in your county would be considered the Kingdom of God. It is the influence of Washington D.C. in your county.

So, everything that D.C. is saying, that county federal building can enforce because it has federal standing in that county. Anytime you want to deal with the federal government, you do it through that building. Why? Because that building carries the influence of D.C. Arrests and prosecutions can happen in the federal building in your county. Binding and loosing can happen. There are cases that can be filed there and there are courts with trials and judges.

> *Jesus came to restore the Kingdom of God on earth.*

The Kingdom of God in heaven would be like D.C. in this scenario. We would be like that governing influence. Jesus has come to restore to earth the Kingdom of God, the government of heaven. You and I are that federal building on the earth.

The ekklesia is that representation of the Kingdom of God. We call it the Kingdom of God on earth. So, when we want to do things on the earth, we have to understand that we are not the source, but we are connected to the source. And the source has given us the authority to do what we do in the earth. We are representing D.C. when we are doing things in our counties through a federal building, and we represent heaven when we are doing things here in the earth. And everything we do here, in the earth, has to be tied to what is being done in heaven to make it legal. You cannot just do your own thing. You can't just create your own church or your own denomination, or your own movement. It has to all come from the home country, heaven. We as ambassadors and citizens are listening, hearing and seeing what Father wants done in heaven. That is what Jesus said in Matthew 6 when he instructed us to pray.

> *Your kingdom come.*
> *Your will be done,*
> *On earth as it is in heaven.*
>
> Matthew 6:10

God's kingdom come. God's will be done. Let the intent of God's heart be manifested here on earth.

How is that actually going to happen? It's going to happen through ambassadors. It is going to happen through sons and daughters who walk in this governmental position as ambassadors, as influencers in a foreign nation for our home nation.

Jesus came to restore the laws of heaven. What are the laws of heaven? There are a lot of them. Most of what is taught in scripture are universal laws because they come from the creator of the universe. God didn't just make up a bunch of rules for earth. To become kingdom people, we must learn the ways of the kingdom. Folks, it goes way beyond earth.

Religion says living by laws is bad, even though it inspires us to live by the law. "Don't do this. Don't touch that." Religion says laws are boundaries that keep us in bondage, and we don't need the laws we find in the Bible. In the Kingdom of God, laws are freedom. They bring liberty. Why? Because law creates culture.

STEWARDSHIP

What does diplomatic status give us? It gives us certain rights and authority. More than that, however, it gives us responsibilities. It requires stewardship of the rank we carry as ambassadors. We must ensure that the things we do on the earth fulfill the will of our home nation, not the nation we are working in. That is why it's illegal for an ambassador of heaven to coexist with other cultures.

> *Do not be mismatched with unbelievers; for what do righteousness and lawlessness share together, or what does light have in common with darkness? Or what harmony does Christ have with Belial, or what does a believer share with an unbeliever? Or what agreement does the temple of God have with idols?*
>
> 2 Corinthians 6:14-16

Ambassadors carry diplomatic ranking in foreign lands. We are in this world structure, but we are not of it. Religion says we are different because we are saved. No. We are different because we are government officials. Our rights and responsibilities are from a governmental structure and order.

AUTHORITY

Our authority has been given to us by the home nation (heaven). This world does not determine our level of authority. God determines that. We are not defined by the world. Therefore, when dealing with struggles in our life, we should not succumb to the prevailing attitudes of survival and poverty.

From my visits to Joan's family in the Philippines, I know that Ambassadors don't ride around in jeepneys. A jeepney is a jeep that's been stretched on the back end so it can fit 15 Americans or 85 Filipinos. They hang off the side. They cling to the top. Pigs are tied onto it. Roosters, too. How those things stay upright is anybody's guess.

In other places, they're called tap-taps. That's what you do to make them stop so you can jump off—you bang on the roof. That's public transportation in the Philippines. Ambassadors don't ride tap-taps. They ride in Land Rovers, Lincolns, and Mercedes G-Wagons blacked out and bullet proof. They inhabit majestic vehicles. Why? Because their transportation is not dictated by the host country. It's determined by their home country. America can afford G-Wagons for their diplomats. They don't put them in jeepneys.

> *We are government officials. Our rights and responsibilities are from a governmental structure and order.*

Religion has dumbed and dulled us with a poverty mentality. Loving our fellow human means being in the same rut as everybody else in the world. If you have anything better, it's unholy.

Folks, that is a religious lie. Our provision, our wealth and our protection are determined by God's kingdom. God is a good giver.

In the Philippines, the Philippine National Police does not guard the U.S. Embassy. The U.S. Marine Corps does that. It's the same throughout the world. When we are in Zimbabwe, we don't see Zimbabwe police guarding the U.S. Embassy. They may partner in some aspects, but the Marines are in charge. Good thing, too. They have resources that the host nation lacks.

The Marines have communications that can summon an aircraft carrier. Warplanes can fill the skies at a moment's notice. I know our record in this regard is not perfect, but America stands strong at its embassies.

The Ambassador is not an elected official. They are an appointed official backed by the nation that appoints them. Therefore, they cannot be fired by the host country. Their position can only be determined by the home country.

When we are born-again, we became ambassadors of heaven. That is why we don't negotiate with demonic strongholds. We destroy them. We don't reason with savages; we conquer savages. We take back the property that belongs to the king. We evict the illegal squatters of the unseen realm. Our battle is not with people but against powers and principalities. This is government. This is governmental authority. This is the Kingdom of God on earth as it is in heaven.

> *Put on the full armor of God, so that you will be able to stand firm against the schemes of the devil. For our struggle is not against flesh and blood, but against the rulers, against the powers, against the world forces of this darkness, against the spiritual forces of wickedness in the heavenly places.*
>
> Ephesians 6:11-12

DIPLOMATIC IMMUNITY

Ambassadors have diplomatic immunity. The local government does not have authority over them. If they carry a black diplomatic passport, they can't be arrested. The host country can't hold them or charge them. Ambassadors can't be put in local prisons. Why? Because you can't arrest a country. You can't jail a nation. The ambassador embodies the nation. Even their family has diplomatic immunity. Now, an ambassador can be recalled for egregious behavior. For Born-again Believers, being recalled means we go back to the home country of heaven and wait for the resurrection.

Diplomatic immunity is a powerful concept when applied to the Kingdom of God. Consider some of the protections we are promised.

> *Behold, I have given you authority to walk on snakes and scorpions, and authority over all the power of the enemy, and nothing will injure you.*
>
> Luke 10:19

> *You are from God, little children, and have overcome them; because greater is He who is in you than he who is in the world.*
>
> John 4:4

Ambassador

> *These things I have spoken to you so that in Me you may have peace. In the world you have tribulation, but take courage; I have overcome the world.*
>
> John 16:32

What do we have to worry about? Nothing can touch us. Oh...it can touch us, but it can't prevail against us. We have the power and authority to trample on the heads of serpents, scorpions and all the powers of the enemy. Nothing will harm us. It's not because we have a shield of glory around us. It's because we have diplomatic immunity around us. All of our home country is backing us. Even the enemy knows and respects God's kingdom government.

In Luke 10, Jesus sent out 72 ambassadors with the power and authority of their home country.

What do we have to worry about?

> *Now after this the Lord appointed seventy-two others, and sent them in pairs ahead of Him to every city and place where He Himself was going to come.*
>
> Luke 10:1

They cast out devils and healed the sick. Notice that they did all of that before the death, resurrection and ascension of Jesus. They were not even born-again. They were what seeker-sensitive people like to call "pre-Christians." They were in the process of becoming born-again Christians. But they were with the King and he conferred upon them kingdom authority. They certainly enjoyed it!

> *Now the seventy-two returned with joy, saying, "Lord, even the demons are subject to us in Your name!"*
>
> *And He said to them, "I watched Satan fall from heaven like lightning. Behold, I have given you authority to walk on snakes and scorpions, and authority over all the power of the enemy, and nothing will injure you. Nevertheless, do not*

rejoice in this, that the spirits are subject to you, but rejoice that your names are recorded in heaven."

Luke 10:17-20

Jesus summed it up nicely: "Look, don't be so excited about that. Here's what you need to be excited about, that your name is recorded in Heaven."

What did he say? The good news that our names are recorded in heaven does not mean: "Rejoice because you are saved and you get to go to heaven when you die." Jesus was saying: "Rejoice that you are a citizen of the Kingdom of God. Your citizenship is not in this world. It's in another world. It's in another governmental structure. It's in another country which gives you power in this one. That's why you could do all that cool stuff."

> *The enemy can't touch us. He has no power over us because we have diplomatic immunity.*

So, how can we invade the space of someone else when we are in their country? How can we impose who we are on another sovereign nation? Well, it happens every day. God has raised up a nation in the earth that demonstrates this well. It is the United States of America. The U.S. has implied power in nations that we don't rule. We have influence, great influence. Some call it manipulative influence. We are not perfect. Yet we have influence in most nations around the world because of our strength and power. Nations have been overturned by the word of our president. Leaders have been disposed and governments upended because one of our high officials ordered the change. Some of it worked out well; some of it did not.

When viewed through certain lenses today, we might think that's not right. We shouldn't be doing those things. I'm not writing this to defend everything the United States has done. Rather, I'm drawing an example back to where you and I are from—the Kingdom of God. We go into other governmental structures—those ruled by demonic strongholds—and we overturn them as sons and daughters of the King. We actually replace leadership. We effect a change in the allegiance of the populace. They're no longer loyal to nations that have controlled them in the past. Now they are loyal to the Kingdom of God because they've been converted.

This is our approach to life and ministry in our communities, cities and nations. The ekklesia is instituting kingdom leadership. We are not trying to get a bunch of folks to heaven. We are there trying to get heaven to a bunch of folks. That was Jesus's command.

> *Our Father, who is in heaven,*
> *Hallowed be Your name.*
> *Your kingdom come,*
> *Your will be done,*
> *On earth as it is in heaven.*
>
> Matthew 6:9-10

We pray for God's will to be done on this colony of earth. This is not a post-rapture, post-tribulation idea. This is a now idea. Jesus emphatically stated that the kingdom was imminent within a generation of his presence.

> *And Jesus was saying to them, "Truly I say to you, there are some of those who are standing here who will not taste death until they see the kingdom of God when it has come with power."*
>
> Mark 9:1

This is why the concept of diplomatic immunity is important when operating in enemy territory, recruiting people for what God has put in our hearts to do. The enemy can't touch us. He has no power over us because we have diplomatic immunity. We are of high rank, diplomatic agents from the sovereign nation that sponsors us.

This changes our approach to everything. Whatever challenges our territory is crossing Heaven's territory. If you've established your city as a place where the Kingdom of God is, then that city, whether they like it or not, belongs to the Kingdom of God. How? By the declaration of your words.

Joan and I pray like this:

> Franklin, Tennessee belongs to the Kingdom of God. We take this territory for the kingdom. We take surrounding regions for God. Nashville is for the Kingdom of God. Through our diplomatic authority from our home nation, we declare that the state of Tennessee belongs to the Kingdom of God.
>
> We will see things change as we carry out prayer assignments around this nation. It's an invasion of diplomats and kings. Nothing can stop it.

Since we and others have been praying like this, there have been many kingdom-minded ministries move to our area. Here is an assignment for your area. Drive around your city limits and make declarations over your city. You may need to drive around your city. Take someone with you. Have one driver and one declarer. Start declaring what you want to happen in your region.

As we act on what God puts in our hearts, we tap into the resources of heaven. If your dad owned Exxon, and he told you to drive the family across the country for summer vacation, do you think you'd pay for gas? Still, if you refused the assignment, you'd never tap into that reserve in the first place.

ALLIANCES

In the world, we make alliances with other nations. We exchange ambassadors, build embassies, loosen trade and draw up treaties for cross-cultural exchanges and protection. In olden days, we even traded our children in marriage to make the bond stronger. (Great for the countries, not so great for the kids.) In all these things, the nations remain independent. In the Kingdom of God, however, nations don't remain independent. They become property of the King. That is why Jesus said in Matthew:

Go, therefore, and make disciples of all the nations, baptizing them in the name of the Father and the Son and the Holy Spirit, teaching them to follow all that I commanded you; and behold, I am with you always, to the end of the age

Matthew 28:19-20

Go and make disciples of nations doesn't mean just teach them the ways of God, but impart kingdom culture, saturate them with influence, lead them to God by way of his kingdom. As hungry hearts respond to the Spirit of God, we will see nations of the earth transformed to resemble heaven. We are experiencing that today. Religion says it can't happen. Kingdom says it is happening. Jesus instructs us to make disciples of nations, bringing them into alignment and allegiance with the Kingdom of God...as it is in heaven.

Protection

Impart kingdom culture, saturate them with influence, lead them to God by way of his kingdom.

Embassies in foreign countries offer protection to citizens of that embassy. If Joan or I, for example, are anywhere in the world where America has an Embassy. We can go to the embassy for help and be protected. There are many cases of people being threatened by other governments who take refuge in an embassy. Embassies operate like microcosms of their home country. They are sovereign territory.

Representatives

Diplomats are expected to be stellar examples of the nation they represent. In like manner, we need to present the Kingdom of God in a fair and favorable light. Americans tend to Americanize every country they encounter. We hold up the example of democracy as a good thing, but it doesn't work in every country. It's not designed to work with every country's culture.

Not so, the Kingdom of God. Present and convert is exactly what we are called to do. We seek to transplant our culture to other people and nations. But we do it nicely. Love does not force-feed. The beautiful part is that living the gospel makes people hungry to be like we are. Let's face it. If they don't like what they see, no amount of persuasion is going to change them, unless a mob of raging natives burning us at the stakes counts as being on fire for God.

Handled properly, there will be no successful resistance to the message we embody. Remember from chapter two: one plants, another waters, and God gives the increase. We have to be patient, careful and authentic. The Bible says that people actually try to force themselves into the Kingdom of God.

> *And from the days of John the Baptist until now the kingdom of heaven has been treated violently, and violent men take it by force.*
>
> Matthew 11:12

There's a liberty that comes with the Kingdom of God. People and nations know when they need God. They just don't know what the answer looks like...until we show up. Religion engenders resistance and persecution. Eventually people get tired of it. But kingdom brings life. It's hard to turn that away. People just want it and they can't explain why.

Despite propaganda to the contrary, most of the world still looks to the United States to bring good things. They want that influence in their land. They expect us to always take the high road and do what's right and good. It's the same with the Kingdom of God. Much of what it means to be an ambassador comes down to simple acts of kindness.

> *And whoever gives one of these little ones just a cup of cold water to drink in the name of a disciple, truly I say to you, he shall by no means lose his reward.*
>
> Matthew 10:42

Ambassador

True spirituality that is pure in the eyes of our Father God is to make a difference in the lives of the orphans, and widows in their troubles, and to refuse to be corrupted by the world's values.

James 1:27 TPT

> *Kingdom brings life. It's hard to turn that away.*

America does all it can to be a positive force in the countries that it operates. Marines and other embassy personnel play a major role in fostering goodwill overseas. You will see them digging wells, setting up hospital tents and operating heavy machinery when natural disasters happen. The Marines can also be counted on to conduct boot-polishing classes! They're in there, doing good for people who are not citizens of America. That is what we are called to do, both as Americans and as Kingdom citizens. For us to know to do good and yet to not do it, that is sin.

If anyone, then, knows the good they ought to do and doesn't do it, it is sin for them.

James 4:17 NIV

As kingdom citizens, you and I are required to do good to people who are not yet citizens of the Kingdom of God. Our actions speak so much louder than our words.

Preach the gospel at all times. When necessary, use words.

St. Francis

Let us and our nation of heaven be greeted with joy, expectation, even jealousy of wanting to be a kingdom citizen. Much of the world looks up to us. I've seen the joy on the faces of impoverished people who are receiving goods and services "Courtesy of the People of the United States." It's powerful.

In the Philippines, Mount Pinatubo exploded in 1991. Personnel at Clark Air Base and other bases around the nation came to aid the country.

There is a reason why our southern border is crushed with immigrants. People are desperate for work, for freedom. Those who are here illegally don't want to return to their country because they've learned to enjoy this way of life. They will do anything to stay here.

The same thing should be happening in the Kingdom of God. People from other theological nations should be clamoring at our proverbial borders. Have you ever noticed that we refer to the Nation of Islam, not the Religion of Islam? They have a concept of government and authority in their structure. The world's religions will question what they believe when they see the good in us that they don't see in their religion. Why? Because when they see us, they're not looking at another religion. They're looking at a kingdom that can provide what their religion promised but never delivered.

We need to exercise our rights and responsibility as ambassadors, sons and daughters, and kings. These three major titles define us. Each of them carries a different influence and authority, but they are all focused on our home country of heaven. Hallelujah!

5

Influence

From that time Jesus began to preach and say, "Repent, for the kingdom of heaven is at hand."

Matthew 4:17

THE ORIGINAL DIVINE PURPOSE OF GOD was to establish a community of heavenly citizens on earth, thereby extending the culture of heaven on earth. This paralleled the ekklesia in the Roman world. It was their responsibility to enter a conquered city and change its culture to Roman.

The mission of Jesus was, *and is*, to restore the earth to the Kingdom of God, bearing the likeness of the culture of heaven.

THE POWER OF CITIZENSHIP

In this chapter, I'll be teaching from a passage in Acts. What follows is a retelling of an episode from the adventures of the Apostle Paul as he endeavored to bring the Kingdom of God to the Jews—a people who thought of themselves, and only themselves, as that kingdom. First, the official version:

> *When the seven days were almost over, the Jews from Asia, upon seeing him in the temple, began to stir up all the crowd and laid hands on him [Paul], crying out, "Men of Israel, help! This is the man who instructs everyone everywhere*

against our people and the Law and this place; and besides, he has even brought Greeks into the temple and has defiled this holy place!"

For they had previously seen Trophimus the Ephesian in the city with him, and they thought that Paul had brought him into the temple. Then the whole city was provoked, and the people rushed together, and taking hold of Paul they dragged him out of the temple, and immediately the doors were shut. While they were intent on killing him, a report came up to the commander of the Roman cohort that all Jerusalem was in confusion. He immediately took along some soldiers and centurions and ran down to the crowd; and when they saw the commander and the soldiers, they stopped beating Paul. Then the commander came up and took hold of him and ordered that he be bound with two chains; and he began asking who he was and what he had done. But among the crowd, some were shouting one thing and some another, and when he could not find out the facts because of the uproar, he ordered that Paul be brought into the barracks. When Paul got to the stairs, it came about that he was carried by the soldiers because of the violence of the mob; for the multitude of people kept following them, shouting, "Away with him!"

As Paul was about to be brought into the barracks, he said to the commander, "May I say something to you?"

And he said, "Do you know Greek? Then you are not the Egyptian who some time ago stirred up a revolt and led the four thousand men of the Assassins out into the wilderness?"

But Paul said, "I am a Jew of Tarsus in Cilicia, a citizen of no insignificant city; and I beg you, allow me to speak to the people."

Influence

> *When he had given him permission, Paul, standing on the stairs, motioned to the people with his hand; and when there was a great silence, he spoke to them in the Hebrew dialect...*
>
> Acts 21:27-40

The set up is that Paul went to Jerusalem and met with the council in Jerusalem, and a hit was put out on him. The religious leadership were very upset with Paul, and they grew livid when they thought he brought a Greek into the temple. This, in their minds, defiled their holy place.

The story picks up with Paul in the temple. The Jewish leaders grabbed Paul and loudly accused him of everything from defiling the temple, robbing the collection plates, breaking 12 of the 10 Commandments, to violating the local building code. Their vocal accusations worked as intended; the entire city was provoked. A crowd formed, rushed together, dragged Paul out of the temple, and immediately the temple doors were shut behind him. As they kicked and punched and called Paul terrible names, a report came up to the commander of the Roman cohort that all Jerusalem was in a riot.

The commander rounded up some soldiers and centurions and headed downtown. Remember what a centurion was? A man over a hundred men. This commander took several of those with him and raced to the riot. When the bloodthirsty crowd saw the commander and his hundreds armed to the teeth, they stopped beating Paul. Probably a good choice on their part.

Not knowing what else to do, the commander ordered Paul to be bound with chains as the instigators in the crowd continued to scream accusations against Paul.

> *But among the crowd, some were shouting one thing and some another, and when he could not find out the facts because of the uproar, he ordered him to be brought into the barracks. When he got to the stairs, he was carried by the soldiers because of the violence of the mob; for the*

> *multitude of the people kept following them, shouting, "Away with him!"*
>
> *As Paul was about to be brought into the barracks, he said to the commander, look at this story, "May I say something to you?"*
>
> *And he said, "Do you know Greek? Then you are none of the Egyptians who some time ago stirred up a riot and led the four thou men of the Assassins out of the wilderness?"*
>
> *But Paul said, "I am a Jew of Tarsus, a citizen of no insignificant city."*
>
> Acts 21:34-39

Paul had a plan, and he began to execute it. "I am a Jew of..." what? Tarsus. He identified himself as "a citizen of no insignificant city." In essence: "I belong to a city of great influence."

Notice that Paul's emphasis was not on his religion, it was on his citizenship.

> *"I beg of you, allow me to speak to the people."*
>
> *When he had given him permission, Paul, standing on the stairs, motioned to the people with his hand; and when there was a great silence, he spoke to them in the Hebrew dialect, saying...*
>
> Acts 21:39-40

What was Paul doing? He's got a bunch of Pharisees and Sadducees inflaming a crowd ready to kill him. But he declared that he is a Jew and a citizen from a very significant city. Then Paul spoke to them in the local dialect. He was demonstrating the power of citizenship, but in a way that the locals would understand. He was being authentic.

> *"Brothers and fathers, hear my defense which I now offer to you."*
>
> *And when they heard that he was addressing them in the Hebrew dialect, they became even more quiet; and he said,*

"I am a Jew, born in Tarsus of Cilicia, but brought up in this city, educated under Gamaliel, strictly according to the Law of our fathers, being zealous for God just as you all are today. I persecuted this Way to the death, binding and putting both men and women into prisons, as also the high priest and all the Council of the elders can testify. From them I also received letters to the brothers, and started off for Damascus in order to bring even those who were there to Jerusalem as prisoners to be punished.

Acts 22:1-5

> *Paul was demonstrating the power of citizenship, but in a way that the locals would understand. He was being authentic.*

Let's look at what Paul told the people. "Brethren and fathers, hear my defense which now I offer to you." He's establishing relationship with the crowd.

"And when they heard that he was addressing them in the Hebrew dialect, they became even more quiet." They began to listen. Why? Because he tapped into their culture, a culture that he knew well.

"I am a Jew, born in Tarsus, brought up in this city, educated under Gamaliel, strictly according to the law of our fathers, being zealous for God just as you all are today."

There's a couple of things here. Paul dropped words and names which gave him status. He was saying, "I am a Jew; I am a Hebrew; I am a citizen of Tarsus," which was one of the most influential cities in that region. Further, Paul said: "I was educated under Gamaliel," which was the most prestigious school in the whole nation. This school was not a public school; it was a private school. You had to have money to go there. Paul was from a very rich family. No wonder, as he dropped his credentials, that the crowd was silenced.

Let me tell you something. When you step into a place and give your credentials, things will quiet down. Why? Because you come from a place of influence and prestige. You come from the greatest nation in the universe—the Kingdom of God.

As you stand before crowds and forces arrayed against you, seeking to kill you, kill your message and your influence, you can say, "I am from the nation of all nations. I am a citizen of the city of all cities. Hear what I'm about to tell you." And in doing so, there will be an authority and curiosity released. People will stop long enough to judge your authenticity from the next thing that comes out of your mouth. Better make it good.

CREDENTIALS

Let's take a quick detour to learn about some Jews who didn't pass the authenticity test. Again, from the book of Acts:

> *Then some of the itinerant Jewish exorcists undertook to invoke the name of the Lord Jesus over those who had evil spirits, saying, "I adjure you by the Jesus whom Paul proclaims." Seven sons of a Jewish high priest named Sceva were doing this. But the evil spirit answered them, "Jesus I know, and Paul I recognize, but who are you?" And the man in whom was the evil spirit leaped on them, mastered all of them and overpowered them, so that they fled out of that house naked and wounded.*
>
> Acts 19:13-16

This is what is known in the hallowed halls of academia as The Seven Stupid Sons of Sceva. They found a man possessed by a devil, and they said, "Come out of him in the name of Jesus, whom Paul preaches."

Now, they at least had the good sense to use "whom" instead of "who," but unfortunately, they did not have ambassador authority through citizenship to challenge this evil spirit. They didn't know that, but the demon did.

"Jesus I know, and Paul I recognize, but who are you?"

Influence

Actually, a better translation is: "Jesus, we know. Paul, we are getting to know."

In essence: "Paul has started to bring us the same trouble that his Secretary of State, Jesus, brought us. But we don't know you seven fools."

> *People will stop long enough to judge your authenticity from the next thing that comes out of your mouth. Better make it good.*

The possessed guy then jumped up and beat them silly, tore off their clothes and sent them running. You could say they failed at deliverance ministry, so they started a naked ministry instead. First Church of the Naked Neophytes.

Why did things go so wrong for the Stupid Seven? It wasn't that they weren't saved. Here's our clue. The reaction of the demon was not a religious reaction, it was a governmental reaction. He was saying, "I have authority here. I've encountered Jesus. And we are encountering the authority that Paul brings. But you carry no authority. You are not one of them. Therefore, you have no power over us."

Clearly, the demonic power recognized governmental power. We also see this from Matthew.

> *And when He [Jesus] came to the other side into the country of the Gadarenes, two demon-possessed men confronted Him as they were coming out of the tombs. They were so extremely violent that no one could pass by that way. And they cried out, saying, "What business do You have with us, Son of God? Have You come here to torment us before the time?"*
>
> Matthew 8:28-29

When the demons asked what Jesus' business was with them, they were not making a religious inquiry. We don't read: "Why are you here to negotiate with us before the time?" There was no negotiation involved here. If you are reading the King James version, it says,

> And, behold, they cried out, saying, What have we to do with thee, Jesus, thou Son of God? Art thou come hither to torment us before the time?

Anytime you hear *thee, thou* and *art* together in one speech, you know things are about to get biblical.

Now yes, later in the story, the demons begged to be allowed to enter a nearby herd of swine, and Jesus allowed it.

> Now there was a herd of many pigs feeding at a distance from them. And the demons begged Him, saying, "If You are going to cast us out, send us into the herd of pigs." And He said to them, "Go!" And they came out and went into the pigs; and behold, the whole herd rushed down the steep bank into the sea and drowned in the waters.
>
> Matthew 8:30-32

Notice, however, that this was not a negotiation where each party gives up something to reach an agreement. Jesus was always in charge. Those demons were coming out whether they identified as pigs or not. Jesus was there to enforce one contract and dissolve another.

As we are told in 1 John:

> The one who practices sin is of the devil; for the devil has been sinning from the beginning. The Son of God appeared for this purpose, to destroy the works of the devil.
>
> 1 John 3:8

Dealing with the demons in the possessed men was just one way that Jesus exercised governmental authority to destroy the work of the devil. Jesus didn't do a religious act to cast out devils. He was the government. He just as well could have said, "In the name of ME! Come out!"

Religious people can also cast out demons, but they can't keep them out of the person. Worse, the demons usually bring friends when they return. Why? Because the delivered person remains in the context of religion. They don't understand the governmental rights of a believer, and so they have no basis for remaining free. They need to learn what freedom really is. Freedom is not sleeping late on Sunday morning because you don't have usher duty. Freedom is looking bondage dead in the eye and realizing you don't belong there anymore. You're free.

Whenever we cast a devil out of somebody based on governmental authority, we have the ability to bring that person into the kingdom, establishing them as sons and daughters. The enemy can't return because the house is filled. It now has a throne and a king occupying it, ruling and reigning with purpose.

Citizenship in the kingdom brings authority, not membership. Religion confers membership. We are not members; we are citizens. Membership restricts us through religion. Citizenship empowers us through national identity. Glory to God!

Citizenship brings authority... It empowers us through national identity.

Let's jump back to Paul's endeavors to share his testimony with a raging crowd intent on making him a martyr. As you recall, the Roman commander just granted Paul permission to speak. Paul started in the Hebrew dialect, and the crowd was silenced. Here's part of what Paul told them.

I persecuted this Way to the death, binding and putting both men and women into prisons, as also the high priest and all the Council of the elders can testify. From them I also received letters to the brothers, and started off for Damascus in order to bring even those who were there to Jerusalem as prisoners to be punished. "But it happened that as I was on my way, approaching

> *Damascus at about noon, a very bright light suddenly flashed from heaven all around me, and I fell to the ground and heard a voice saying to me, 'Saul, Saul, why are you persecuting Me?*
>
> Acts 22:4-7

Paul was offering them his testimony, one that had the power to convert the entire Jewish nation, a nation that, at that very moment, was under the iron grip of Roman oppression. The Jews were being offered freedom...again. And just as they did with Jesus, they cried "Away with such a man...!"

> *They listened to him up to this statement, and then they raised their voices and said, "Away with such a man from the earth, for he should not be allowed to live!"*
>
> Acts 22:22

Religion is a wicked force. It wasn't the crowd of Jews who wanted to kill Paul. They didn't even know Paul. They were raging against what they had been told Paul represented. It was their religious leaders who wanted to kill Paul. They needed the crowd...and the Romans...to do it for them.

> *And as they were shouting and throwing off their cloaks and tossing dust into the air.*
>
> Acts 22:23

Can you imagine this scene? These people were tormented; they had demonic religious manifestations. They may have succeeded in killing Paul, but the forces of death driving them would have slowly destroyed them over time. Fortunately, God had other ideas for Paul.

> *The commander ordered that he [Paul] be brought into the barracks, saying that he was to be interrogated by flogging so that he would find out the reason why they were shouting against him that way. But when they stretched him out with straps, Paul said to the centurion who was*

Influence

> *standing by, "Is it lawful for you to flog a man who is a Roman and uncondemned?"*
>
> Acts 22:24-25

Get the picture here. They stretched out Paul with leather thongs tied to his arms and legs. Paul didn't say anything. He let them tie him to this torture rack. He was waiting. The centurion who was standing by was thinking, *This is one more trouble-making Jew. I can do anything I want to this guy.* But he was about to find out how wrong he was.

Paul said to the centurion, "Is it lawful for you to scourge a man who is a Roman and uncondemned?"

Paul was invoking his citizenship. It was not Paul's education that got the attention of the centurion, it was his question. "Is it lawful to scourge, to beat an un-condemned Roman citizen?" Things were heating up. From Acts 22:26:

"Is it legal for you to flog a Roman citizen who hasn't even been found guilty?" (NIV)

When the centurion heard this, he went to the commander and told him, saying, "What are you about to do? For this man is a Roman."

In other words, "You're fixin' to make the mistake of all mistakes. You aren't beating a Jew. The religious Jews are accusing him, but this man has stepped into our world, and now he is asking questions about our culture, our government, and our treatment because he's claiming to be a Roman."

Paul could work it, couldn't he? He had the Jewish leaders enraged, the crowd inflamed, and the Roman centurion shaking in his sandals.

> *The commander came and said to Paul, "Tell me, are you a Roman?"*
>
> *And he said, "Yes."*
>
> Acts 22:27

Citizenship cannot be identified by the color of our skin. It's not the clothes we wear. Not even the cars we drive. It is identified by the culture that we keep.

"'Tell me, are you a Roman?"

"Yes.'"

The commander of the centurion said, "Are you a Roman citizen? Are you gonna get us in trouble?"

"Yes, I am a Roman. I am uncondemned. I'm also a Jew, and I know a few good lawyers."

The commander was stunned.

> *The commander answered, "I acquired this citizenship for a large sum of money." And Paul said, "But I was actually born a citizen."*
>
> Acts 22:28

The Roman commander said to Paul, "I'm a Roman too, but I got my citizenship by purchasing it for a large sum of money."

In those days, you could buy Roman citizenship if you were rich enough. Paul already identified his wealth by saying he was schooled by Gamaliel. Only the wealthy went there. Paul's father was a very wealthy merchant and businessman. He traded with the Romans in Israel and other nations. He had great influence and was able to become a Roman.

By comparing citizenships, Paul was letting the commander know, "My citizenship trumps your citizenship."

A purchased citizenship gave you a class, but when you were born a Roman citizen, it put you above those who bought their citizenships. Paul said, "You might have paid for yours, but I was born into mine. My daddy bought his, but I am a Roman because I was born to a Roman citizen."

Paul's example to us is this: When you are born-again, you can look at a principality or demonic stronghold over a region, and when they begin to question your standing, you can say, "No, I didn't buy my citizenship. I am not doing religious acts to get heaven to like me. This is not penance. I'm not working off my sins. I'm born of the country of heaven. I'm related to that nation by a shared bloodline with Jesus. I didn't pay. My daddy is the king. I am a king under him."

As citizens of the kingdom, we stand in an expanding territory out of inherent right. Why? Because "the earth is the Lord's, and the fullness thereof" (Psalm 24:1). And what is the Lord's is ours.

Is it legal…?

The kingdom that was in the world back when Adam had control, all belonged to the Father. Everything. Even the worlds and the kingdoms, the governmental structures in the earth, they all belong to God, but they're not all in God's hands. You and I are to go and bring them back into the hands of our king.

So, when we stand and face a demonic stronghold, we are not there to war with it. We are there to subdue it. We are not there to have a violent confrontation with it. We are there as a representative of the Kingdom of God to bring it into subjection to our king. It can choose to come peacefully, or it can lose everything its got…and it will.

Think about that. Religion doesn't give us this opportunity. Religion does not afford us this power and authority. Kingdom does. Kingdom gets respect as it did for Paul.

> *And Paul said, "But I was actually born a citizen." Therefore, those who were about to interrogate him immediately backed away from him; and the commander also was afraid when he found out that he was a Roman, and because he had put him in chains.*
>
> Acts 22:28-29

Paul said here, "I was actually born a citizen." Therefore, those who were about to examine him immediately let him go. This word, *examine*, means "to look into who he was, to get between him and reality to look for fault." So, they weren't going to look for fault within him or try to change his reality. Instead, they immediately let him go. Even the commander was afraid when he realized he had put a Roman in chains.

This is the power of citizenship. If Paul's Roman citizenship could do that for him, how much more can your citizenship in the Kingdom of God do for you?

Paul's torturers immediately halted. They obeyed government authority conveyed through Roman citizenship. We can experience the same.

When we find ourselves in situations of unjust assault and persecution, we know what to say. "Is this legal? In light of the death, burial, resurrection, ascension and enthronement of Jesus at the right hand of the Father, and Holy Spirit coming into the earth, is it legal for you demonic forces to do what you're trying to do to me?"

No, it is not legal! Why not? Inherent rights of Citizenship! Glory to God!

6

Boundaries

THE APOSTLE PAUL had his strengths and weaknesses, but many of his qualities—like all of us—were neither. They were simply the man himself, standing as a citizen of the kingdom, proclaiming the truth of God and not giving a rip who it offended. Sometimes that worked better than other times.

> *Now looking intently at the Council, Paul said, "Brothers, I have lived my life with an entirely good conscience before God up to this day." But the high priest Ananias commanded those standing beside him to strike him on the mouth.*
>
> Acts 23:1-2

The situation described here began in Acts 21. From our study in the previous chapter, we know that Paul was apprehended by a violent mob in Jerusalem. Urged on by Jewish leaders, the crazed crowd nearly killed him until the Roman army showed up, apprehended Paul, and hauled him off for interrogation. They were about to torture the truth out of him when Paul declared his Roman citizenship, and they wisely decided to let him be. The next morning proceeded like this:

> *Now on the next day, wanting to know for certain why Paul had been accused by the Jews, he [the commander] released him and ordered the chief priests and all the*

> *Council to assemble, and he brought Paul down and placed him before them.*
>
> Acts 22:30

It was before this council that Paul received the crack across the jaw. How would you like to be in that scenario? Paul said, "I'm living a good life," and they smacked him on the mouth. Guess they didn't like hearing that. Ah, but Paul was just warming up.

> *Then Paul said to him, "God is going to strike you, you whitewashed wall! Do you sit to try me according to the Law, and in violation of the Law, order me to be struck?"*
>
> Acts 23:3

Paul was declaring boundaries. Law is an important part of any nation. That strike created a prophetic environment for him. What Paul was talking about here was the governing boundaries of the situation; the law of the land; the culture. It was one he had to obey as well.

> *But those present said, "Are you insulting God's high priest?" And Paul said, "I was not aware, brothers, that he is high priest; for it is written: 'You shall not speak evil of a ruler of your people.'"*
>
> Acts 23:4-5

Paul's response was accurate for the religious environment he was in, but notice that he brought kingdom principles into it. He used the phrase, "It is written." Now, Paul knew that "it is written" is not a religious phrase. It is a governmental phrase. Paul brought this into the conversation to keep from getting another rap on the lip. But he did it legally. As the council interrogated him, Paul used scripture to his advantage.

> *But Paul, perceiving that one group were Sadducees and the other Pharisees, began crying out in the Council, "Brothers, I am a Pharisee, a son of Pharisees; I am on trial for the hope and resurrection of the dead!" When he said this, a*

> dissension occurred between the Pharisees and Sadducees, and the assembly was divided. For the Sadducees say that there is no resurrection, nor an angel, nor a spirit, but the Pharisees acknowledge them all.
>
> Acts 23:6-8

"Brethren, I am a Pharisee, a son of a Pharisee; I am on trial for the hope and the resurrection of the dead!" Such wisdom!

> And a great uproar occurred; and some of the scribes of the Pharisaic party stood up and started arguing heatedly, saying, "We find nothing wrong with this man; suppose a spirit or an angel has spoken to him?"
>
> And when a great dissension occurred, the commander was afraid that Paul would be torn to pieces by them, and he ordered the troops to go down and take him away from them by force, and bring him into the barracks.
>
> Acts 23:9-10

Paul exposed the fault lines of their religion. He ensnared them in their own conflicting doctrines, setting them upon each other. *Smack your own mouths, brothers!*

RESPONSIBILITY TO THE CAUSE

The Roman commander from Acts 22, who had discovered Paul was a Roman citizen by birth, had an obligation to protect him in this hostile religious situation even though the commander did not ascribe to the religious activity. As Paul debated the Jewish leaders, this commander was there to make sure Paul—as a Roman citizen—would be safe in their midst. Most likely, he was afraid of possible repercussions against him from when he put Paul in chains. *I chained up a Roman citizen in Acts 22 and was getting ready to flog him. I better make sure he gets out of Acts 23 alive. I sure hope somebody writes Acts 24 quickly!*

The power of citizenship caused the Roman commander of Jerusalem—a man who did not even believe in Paul's Jewish heritage nor agree with the Pharisees or Sadducees (or any of the "cees" that were around in those days)—to take responsibility for Paul in this hostile environment.

Your citizenship in the kingdom is important, so when you find yourself in hostile religious situations, don't be afraid to speak what you know, because you have a nation backing you.

> *But on the night immediately following, the Lord stood at his side and said, "Take courage; for as you have solemnly witnessed to My cause at Jerusalem, so you must witness at Rome also."*
>
> Acts 23:11 (NASB 1995)

Don't be afraid to speak what you know, because you have a nation backing you.

This is the perfect picture of kingdom citizenship and responsibility. On the night immediately following Paul's life-threatening drama—when he witnessed to the Jewish nation, of which he was a citizen—the Lord stood by Paul's side and called him to witness of the Kingdom of God in Rome, of which he was also a citizen. Paul had a responsibility to the nation that he was a citizen of, to be a witness of the kingdom cause.

Is There Not A Cause?

Goliath and his four brothers showed up in the land of Judah. David's family was from the tribe of Judah. In our vernacular, they were citizens of Judah. Citizenship conferred certain rights and responsibilities, among them was protection of the borders. David's tribe was also known as the Stone Throwers. David's older brothers took the incursion of Goliath and the Philistines rather personally, so they joined with the army to repel the invaders. But the sight of the spear-toting giant sent shivers down their spines, and they fled for cover.

David, who had been left behind to tend the family farm, was sent with provisions to his brothers on the frontlines. They, along with the rest of the army, were hunkered down in the mighty name of valor hiding behind some rocks.

> *So, David got up early in the morning and left the flock with a keeper and took the supplies and went as Jesse had commanded him. And he came to the entrenchment encircling the camp while the army was going out in battle formation, shouting the war cry. Israel and the Philistines drew up in battle formation, army against army. Then David left the baggage in the care of the baggage keeper and ran to the battle line. And he entered and greeted his brothers. As he was speaking with them, behold, the champion, the Philistine from Gath named Goliath, was coming up from the army of the Philistines, and he spoke these same words; and David heard him.*
>
> 1 Samuel 17:20-23

David heard Goliath and decided he was going to deal with him. Of course, this didn't set well with his brothers.

> *Now Eliab his oldest brother heard him when he spoke to the men; and Eliab's anger burned against David and he said, "Why is it that you have come down? And with whom have you left those few sheep in the wilderness? I myself know your insolence and the wickedness of your heart; for you have come down in order to see the battle."*
>
> *But David said, "What have I done now? Was it not just a question?" Then he turned away from him to another and said the same thing; and the people replied with the same words as before.*
>
> 1 Samuel 17:28-30

In the King James, we have David's retort stated more emphatically.

> And David said, What have I now done? Is there not a cause?
>
> 1 Samuel 17:29

David uttered a rallying cry that resonated throughout the kingdom. "Is there not a cause?" Is there not a kingdom cause? A governmental cause? David was not about to let that uncircumcised Philistine take land that was his inheritance, a land that he was destined to rule. (Even though he didn't know he was going to rule as king; as a citizen, he still took ownership.) Apparently, there was a cause, for David's declaration reached the ears of King Saul.

> *"Is there not a cause?" As citizens of the kingdom, we can answer emphatically, "Yes, there is a cause."*

> Then Saul clothed David with his military attire and put a bronze helmet on his head and outfitted him with armor. And David strapped on his sword over his military attire and struggled at walking, for he had not trained with the armor. So, David said to Saul, "I cannot go with these, because I have not trained with them." And David took them off. Then he took his staff in his hand and chose for himself five smooth stones from the brook and put them in the shepherd's bag which he had, that is, in his shepherd's pouch, and his sling was in his hand; and he approached the Philistine.
>
> I Samuel 17:38-40

Saul tried to dress David in the armor of the day, but David said, "I haven't proven this equipment. I've got to fight with what I've been trained in on the backside of the desert. I'm a stone-thrower. I'm from

Judah, and this giant has invaded Judah. I'll deal with him like my family deals with things. Our motto: Everybody must get stoned."

David picked five smooth stones out of Judah's brook, and he went to face Goliath, the brute who was seeking to enslave his people and take his land. That was not a religious motivation; it was a governmental motivation. It was one nation trying to overcome another nation.

We all know the rest of the story. It was David 1; Giant 0. David went on to trials and tribulations and eventually reigned in Israel. In David's rallying words, we find a timeless lesson. As a citizen of Judah, David declared: "Is there not a cause?" As citizens of the kingdom, we can answer emphatically, "Yes, there is a cause."

The Lord's words to Paul in Acts 23:11 echoed this. Paraphrased, Jesus was saying: "...you have solemnly witnessed to my cause at Jerusalem, so you must witness at Rome also."

The cause continues as citizens of the kingdom go forth against the giants, in Jesus' name.

THE NAME OF JESUS

When we are told of the name of Jesus, it's from scriptures like this:

> *And whatever you ask in My name [Jesus], this I will do, so that the Father may be glorified in the Son.*
>
> John 14:13

> *Until now you have asked for nothing in My name; ask and you will receive, so that your joy may be made full.*
>
> John 16:24

> *Peter said to them, "Repent, and each of you be baptized in the name of Jesus Christ for the forgiveness of your sins; and you will receive the gift of the Holy Spirit.*
>
> Acts 2:38

> *But Peter said, "I do not have silver and gold, but what I do have I give to you: In the name of Jesus Christ the Nazarene, walk!"*
>
> Acts 3:6

> *For this reason also God highly exalted Him, and bestowed on Him the name which is above every name, so that at the name of Jesus every knee will bow, of those who are in heaven and on earth and under the earth, and that every tongue will confess that Jesus Christ is Lord, to the glory of God the Father.*
>
> Philippians 2:9-11

We know that when we say, "in the name of Jesus," it doesn't mean just to say *Jesus*. The phrases, "in my name," or "in the name of..." mean "to buy in, adhere to, and submit to one's cause and one's purpose." The concept here is complete allegiance.

So, when we say "in the name of Jesus," that's not our lucky rabbit's foot. It's not a tag we stick on the end of a prayer to get what we want. It's not the postage stamp that ensures deliverance. *Jesus* is not the security code on the back of our credit cards, the one that's always rubbed out from being slid in and out a hundred times a day.

Yeah, God's gotta answer my prayer now. I put "in the name of Jesus" at the end. Now he's legally bound. "God, YOU said in YOUR Word that...."

No, no, 100 times no. When we use the name of Jesus, it is an acknowledgment that we have bought into his cause, assimilated with his assignment and purpose. It is the stamp on our passports, granting us the rights as citizens to enter and exit at will.

The buy-in is not just intellectual; it is life itself. We have switched citizenships, changed streams, eaten at the tree of life. We've come out of the kingdom of darkness and into the kingdom of light. We understand the meaning of the declaration: Is there not a cause? And we have answered it.

"Jesus, your cause is my cause. Your purpose is my purpose."

That is the born-again experience. Only then do we see the Kingdom of God.

> *Truly, truly, I say to you, unless someone is born again he cannot see the kingdom of God.*
>
> John 3:5

DEFINITIONS OF THE KINGDOM

> *When we use the name of Jesus, it is an acknowledgment that we have bought into his cause, assimilated with his assignment and purpose.*

> *With every prayer and request, pray at all times in the Spirit, and with this in view, be alert with all perseverance and every request for all the saints, and pray in my behalf, that speech may be given to me in the opening of my mouth, to make known with boldness the mystery of the gospel for which I am an ambassador in chains; that in proclaiming it I may speak boldly, as I ought to speak.*
>
> Ephesians 6:18-19

As we say often in these studies, until we understand the definitions of terms, our communication is fruitless. (Unless confusion, disillusion and empty rage are considered fruit.)

The Greek word for *ambassador* is *presbeuo* and means, "to be the elder, to take precedence." So, an Ambassador is an elder, not as in older, but as in an authoritative leader. You might say, "I am not an elder," but that's not true according to this definition. You may not have been appointed an elder in a religious capacity, but if you are an ambassador, you are an elder in the Kingdom of God.

Citizenship According to the Kingdom

The Greek word *ekklesia* means, "an assembly, a congregation." In Greek culture, the *ekklesia* were elders who sat at the gates regulating what entered and exited the city. In other words, they maintained boundaries. "Merchandise in and out? No problem. Just pay the excise tax. Marauding zealots intent on inciting riots? Nope, you can't come in. We already have Greg Hood and his cohorts here. No more zealots need apply."

As citizens of the kingdom, we are ambassadors and elders comprising the ekklesia. We set boundaries and determine what comes in and goes out of the country. The sense is that of a presbytery, which is a group of elders functioning as a regulatory body, but it is more.

Ambassadors are different than the presbyters that we see in 1st Corinthians 12 and Ephesians 4. It's a different makeup, but it has the same principle applied to it as ambassadors entering a region or area. We work together with those that are on assignment with us as elders to determine what we allow in and what we expel.

WHAT DO YOU CONSUME

> *Brothers and sisters, join in following my example, and observe those who walk according to the pattern you have in us. For many walk, of whom I often told you, and now tell you even as I weep, that they are the enemies of the cross of Christ, whose end is destruction, whose god is their appetite, and whose glory is in their shame, who have their minds on earthly things. For our citizenship is in heaven, from which we also eagerly wait for a Savior, the Lord Jesus Christ; who will transform the body of our lowly condition into conformity with His glorious body, by the exertion of the power that He has even to subject all things to Himself.*
>
> Philippians 3:17-21

There were two main groups of people Paul dealt with throughout his ministry—those that were kingdom and those that were religious.

Sometimes it was the Pagan religion, and sometimes it was the Jewish religion, "whose end is destruction, whose god is their appetite, and whose glory is in their shame."

When Paul talks about their appetite or their bellies, he talks about what they consume, what they draw into them. Like the ekklesia at the city gates, Paul was talking about more than just eating food. He was talking about what they drew into their lives, that which seemed to satisfy them spiritually as well as physically. As members of Pagan religions, their source was their demonic gods.

So, the consumption in Paul's admonishment wasn't like having another Ruben sandwich, Jewish rye, hold the pickle. It was not about gluttony. I've heard religion interpret it as such, right before they scheduled the next covered dish supper. In truth, Paul was writing about what people took in at all levels of life.

Recall from chapter 2: The most important choices we make in life are those related to who and what we admit into our lives. To admit is closely related to another word: *believe.*

This is why Jesus stressed "if you believe." The reason is that our belief system changes us. To believe something is to grant access to our innermost being. It's that little window that warns us that some downloaded software wants access to our files, our pictures and all our bank account information, and we click "YES."

When we want to improve our health, we regulate what we admit into our lives. Likewise, when we want to improve our spiritual health, we also regulate what we admit into our lives. We do so by rigorously examining what we believe. To believe that Jesus is Lord is to admit him into our lives. To believe that God loves me is to admit his love into my life. To believe that this man or woman is honorable is to trust them; trust is a belief. I believe they mean well and will do me no harm. Hence, I admit them into my life.

Belief has one more dimension. It actually casts a judgment on whatever we are considering. To believe that someone is the devil incarnate, for example, forms a rigid attitude of judgment about that person; it colors every interaction we have with them. We will now view everything they do through that filter and confirm what we suspected. It's called confirmation bias.

It works in the positive as well. To believe that our grandchildren are perfect little angels means we'll never believe the folks who tell us that, to the contrary, we are presiding over a brood of future rock stars, politicians and robber baron capitalists. (Hey...works for me.)

When we believe that we can do all that God says we can do as citizens and ambassadors of the kingdom, we open ourselves up for to the grace to actually do it. We admit this grace into our lives through our belief. To misuse an old saying: "When you have them by their hearts and minds, the rest will follow."

THE LORD'S INSTRUCTION

Believers love to quote Jesus' prayer in Matthew 6. I do too, but me being me, I prefer to rename it. Calling it the *Lord's Prayer* doesn't quite fit. This is the Lord's instruction to disciples on how to pray, so it would be more fittingly called the *Disciples' Prayer*. If you want the Lord's Prayer, read John 17. That's the real Lord's Prayer. It starts at verse 1:

> *Jesus spoke these things; and raising His eyes to heaven, He said, "Father, the hour has come; glorify Your Son, so that the Son may glorify You…."*

In Matthew 6, Jesus was teaching his disciples to pray. His opening line is revealing. "Our Father who is in Heaven." Every place Jesus referred to the Father, he also gave the Father's geographical location. That's like people introducing me as "Greg Hood, who lives at 1313 Mockingbird Lane, Franklin, Tennessee. In this case, Jesus was introducing the Father who lives "in heaven…."

> *Our Father, who is in heaven,*
> *Hallowed be Your name.*
> *Your kingdom come.*
> *Your will be done,*

Boundaries

On earth as it is in heaven.
Give us this day our daily bread.
And forgive us our debts,
as we also have forgiven our debtors.
And do not lead us into temptation,
but deliver us from evil.

For if you forgive other people for their offenses, your heavenly Father will also forgive you. But if you do not forgive other people, then your Father will not forgive your offenses.

Matthew 6:9-15

> *When we believe that we can do all that God says we can do as citizens and ambassadors of the kingdom, we open ourselves up for to the grace to actually do it.*

So, our Father is where? He is in the home country: heaven. This is an important distinction. Consider: Why is Jesus called the King of kings? And why are we "Special K" kings? Because we're the special kids? No, there's a deeper reason for all this.

In Jesus' culture and timeframe, there could only be one king in a country. There could not be two or more kings in one country, at least not peacefully. If you had two kings in one country for long, it meant a war was underway and somebody was fixin' to lose a trailer.

Kings are territorial. This is why we have the distinction between kings and princes. One king; lots of princes and princesses. Seems to go hand in hand. Put some guy in charge and next thing you know, there's a population explosion. (Go figure.)

Here is a story that explains it well. The King of Portugal took the territory of Brazil so his son could be a king. Any time you are in the same country with your father and your father is the king, you cannot be a king. You are a prince. The father wanted his son to be king, so he acquired the territory and set him as king of Brazil. (Isn't that great?

My father gave me a truck. This guy's father gave him his own country.)

Now the father was still the king of the king (the son). He was the sovereign king over Brazil. The son was the under-king to his dad in Brazil. His father had authority in Brazil, but his son ruled there, not as a prince but as a king. Every time the son returned to Portugal, however, the son would be referred to as the Prince of Portugal. (Personally, I think it would have been a lot simpler if he'd just given the boy a truck.)

CONFERENCE OF POWER

Our kingship is not in heaven even though that is where our citizenship originates. Our kingship is on the earth. Why? Because God gave man authority and dominion in the earth. In reference to the previous story, earth is our Brazil.

So, while we are here, we are kings. When we leave this earth and go back to the home country of heaven, we are no longer kings. I don't know if we'll be called princes or princesses. (That, apparently, is still to be decided in some parts of the country.)

The point is, we are not kings in the presence of the King. Here is what we see from Revelation:

> ...the twenty-four elders will fall down before Him who sits on the throne, and they will worship Him who lives forever and ever, and will cast their crowns before the throne, saying, "Worthy are You, our Lord and our God...."
>
> Revelation 20:10-11

In heaven, there's only one king. On the earth, there are many kings operating in the spheres of influence that God has given them to rule and reign and expand his kingdom.

When Jesus taught his disciples to pray, "Our Father who is heaven...your kingdom come, your will be done on earth as it is in heaven," he was describing a transference of power and authority that was to take place whenever we pray. We are to do in the earthly realm what the Father does in the heavenly realm. This is how power is delegated.

Whenever an ambassador is selected, they're brought before the president. The president does something called "conferring of power." I've seen it done in some nations. They actually lay their hands on the ambassador's shoulders as they kneel. Sometimes the Ambassador puts their hand on a Bible and takes an oath. Either way, authority is passed down by words to this effect: "I confer on you the authority of the United States of America." The ambassador then carries authority of the nation wherever he or she is sent.

Jesus used similar language in the verses below:

> *Fear not, little flock; for it is your Father's good pleasure to <u>give you the kingdom</u>.*
>
> Luke 12:32 KJV

The word *give* is the same Greek word as *confer*.

> *And it shall come to pass in that day, that his burden shall be taken away from off thy shoulder, and his yoke from off thy neck, and <u>the yoke shall be destroyed because of the anointing.</u>*
>
> Isaiah 10:27 KJV

The word *anointing* is not a religious term. Unfortunately, we tend to treat it as such. Whenever we talk about the anointing of God, our voice changes. We get our Pentecostal voice on—a quiet, weighty hush. Folks, let's get real. Saying "the anointing breaks the yolk" is military jargon. The word *anointing* is rooted in the word *coronated*, as in "coronating a king or queen." Coronation is not a religious word. It's a governmental word. What happens whenever someone is coronated? They get a crown, power and authority are conferred, and they are put in charge of a kingdom.

In the Jewish-Hebrew culture, when they spoke of the Messiah, they were not expecting a religious leader but a government leader to restore their kingdom. (A kingdom, I might add, that was lost through their unfaithfulness to God.)

> *So, when they [Jesus' disciples] had come together, they began asking Him, saying, "Lord, is it at this time that You are restoring the kingdom to Israel?"*
>
> Acts 1:6

Jesus is not a religious leader come to establish a religious activity. He is a governmental leader, a king, to establish his kingdom in the earth.

This is heart-rending. All that the disciples have been through, and they are practically begging Jesus to restore the kingdom to Israel. The word *messiah* means "anointed one." They were looking for the one from heaven who would be coronated as their king and lead them out of bondage—specifically bondage to Rome at the time of Jesus. They weren't looking for a high priest, even though Jesus filled that role as well. They were looking for a king, one anointed by heaven to restore their nation—one who ruled from a throne, not one who made sacrifices at an altar.

In a sense, they got both. The priestly anointing we have gives us the right to make things right between ourselves and God. The kingly anointing we have gives us the right to decree what is in heaven onto earth. Both anointings give us authority to do what God has called us to do.

So, in prophesying the Messiah, scripture was not portending a religious leader coming to give us a religious experience. It was an anointed one who will be coronated king over our nation of heaven. He will in turn coronate other kings on earth.

> *He will be great and will be called the Son of the Most High; and the Lord God will give Him the throne of His father David.*
>
> Luke 1:32

Boundaries

For a Child will be born to us, a Son will be given to us;
And the government will rest on His shoulders;
And His name will be called Wonderful Counselor,
Mighty God, Eternal Father, Prince of Peace.
There will be no end to the increase
of His government or of peace
On the throne of David and over his kingdom.

Isaiah 9:6-7

Now, Isaiah was a prophet who wrote extensively about the Messiah. So...has this happened yet? Has Isaiah 9 been fulfilled? Yes. The prophet said that Jesus will sit on the throne of his father, David. It didn't say that he would go into the holy of holies like Aaron. And the government shall be upon the Messiah's shoulders. Not the religion, but the government.

Jesus is not a religious leader come to establish a religious activity. He is a governmental leader, a king, to establish (or re-establish) his kingdom in the earth.

We must stop presenting Jesus as a religious leader. And while we're at it, we must stop referring to the Bible as a religious book. It is not. It is a governmental book. It is a constitution for us. Our leader is a king with a throne and a crown. We cannot mix religion and kingdom. They can't coexist. One overturns the other.

Notice that in the disciples' prayer, Jesus is speaking to God, not begging God.

"Give us this day our daily bread." We know that our provision comes from the Father. Why? Because he's a king. It's his responsibility to provide for his citizens.

"Forgive us of our debts as we also forgive our debtors." This is a provision based on us being willing to forgive people who owe us. (Pro tip: It's not just about money.)

Now, it's not legal in the Kingdom of God for us to charge interest when we loan money to other believers. It's called *usury,* and God forbids it. Sure, we can be concerned about making our money back. Rest assured. You'll get your money...with interest. The king will repay you. He'll give you other avenues for investments. Money will fill your empty pocket. You will be amply provided for.

But you have to be willing to forgive people and let that debt go. Forgiveness doesn't mean "I forgive you." You have to mean it in your heart. Forgiveness is not an emotion; it is a decision. Your emotions will come into alignment with that decision. It is an act of the will. We are to align with that forgiveness and not allow bitterness to dwell in our hearts. If we do not forgive others, then our Father will not forgive us of our transgressions. That's heavy. So, forgive.

Saying: "People owe me money and I'll never get that money" determines our fate. We reap the outcome of our words. So just forgive and let it go. God has much more where that came from. Our financial standing is not determined by the nation in which we live. It is determined by the nation of which we are citizens.

> *Forgiveness is not an emotion; it is a decision.*

"And do not lead us into temptation but deliver us from evil." He is saying, "We know you are going to teach us, but if there's any way to do so without temptation, please do it."

"For yours is the kingdom and the power and glory forever." It never ends. Seasons end. Childhood ends. Even sermons end. (Praise God!) God's kingdom never ends. Amen.

THE LORD'S PRAYER

As we reviewed earlier, John 17 should really be the Lord's Prayer. Here is an excerpt from it; a section pertaining to Ambassadorship.

> *But now I am coming to You; and these things I speak in the world so that they may have My joy made full in themselves. I have given them Your word; and the world has hated them because they are not of the world, just as I am not of the world. I am not asking You to take them out of the world,*

> *but to keep them away from the evil one. They are not of the world, just as I am not of the world. Sanctify them in the truth; Your word is truth. Just as You sent Me into the world, I also sent them into the world. And for their sakes I sanctify Myself, so that they themselves also may be sanctified in truth. I am not asking on behalf of these alone, but also for those who believe in Me through their word, that they may all be one; just as You, Father, are in Me and I in You, that they also may be in Us, so that the world may believe that You sent Me. The glory which You have given Me I also have given to them, so that they may be one, just as We are one; I in them and You in Me, that they may be perfected in unity, so that the world may know that You sent Me, and You loved them, just as You loved Me.*
>
> John 17:13-23

Recall our methods of inquiry. Who was speaking? Jesus. What was he describing? Another order structure. When he was praying the Lord's Prayer, he was essentially saying: "Father, don't take them out of the world. Don't remove them from this place that hates them. Don't remove them from this environment that wants to destroy them, this evil place. Rather, keep them from the evil one. Protect them and cover them as they are in this foreign structure."

This is a perfect example of what it means to be ambassadors.

"They are not of the world, just as I am not of the world. Sanctify them in the truth; Your word is truth."

Why did Jesus tell the Father, "Your word is truth"? Because the words of the king are law; they are the truth. No matter how you see it or how you understand it, God's word is the absolute truth.

Jesus' prayer was not just for the 12 Apostles or the 72 pre-Apostles. He was declaring this for all who would believe in his name. This Lord's Prayer is for everyone who will come into the kingdom by believing in Jesus' name.

"I in them and you in me. That they may be perfected in unity so that the world may know that You sent me and loved them even as You have loved me." Jesus was asking God to sanctify us. Sanctification means several things, but one of the things it refers to is righteousness.

Sanctification is a process. Righteousness is instantaneous when we are born-again. Sanctification is ongoing in our lives as we grow and learn about coming into greater alignment with our nation—the country we are from. Righteousness grants us access to sanctification.

Sanctification is not about things we are being separated from. That is a religious concept. True sanctification is about things that we are, in a greater way, being separated *unto*. In a word: holiness. God sets us in new territory. We are bound by his love. These boundaries designate holiness. We are not holy because of what we don't do. We are holy because of who we are connected to. Religion says we are holy because of what we deny. This is unfortunate. God said we are holy from being connected to Him. His holiness becomes our holiness.

> *True sanctification is about things that we are being separated unto. In a word: holiness.*

But it is due to Him that you are in Christ Jesus, who became to us wisdom from God, and righteousness and sanctification, and redemption...

1 Corinthians 1:30

He made Him who knew no sin to be sin in our behalf, so that we might become the righteousness of God in Him.

2 Corinthians 5:21

BOUNDARIES FROM THE OLD TESTAMENT

We'll end this chapter on boundaries with the declarations of God when he answered Job out of the whirlwind. The first aspects that God identified about himself to the repentant Job were the boundaries he established during creation. Upon further review, God was setting boundaries between himself and Job. Essentially: *I'm God and you're not.*

Addressing the longsuffering and now knee-knocking man, he spoke thusly:

> *Where were you when I laid*
> *the foundation of the earth?*
> *Tell Me, if you have understanding,*
> *Who set its measurements? Since you know.*
> *Or who stretched the measuring line over it?*
> *On what were its bases sunk?*
> *Or who laid its cornerstone,*
> *When the morning stars sang together*
> *And all the sons of God shouted for joy?*
> *Or who enclosed the sea with doors*
> *When it went out from the womb, bursting forth;*
> *When I made a cloud its garment,*
> *And thick darkness its swaddling bands,*
> *And I placed boundaries on it*
> *And set a bolt and doors,*
> *And I said, "As far as this point you shall come,*
> *but no farther;*
> *And here your proud waves shall stop"?*

Job 38:4-11

As citizens of the Kingdom of God, setting boundaries is what we do, because that is what our king does. It is part of the rights and responsibilities that we inherit as sons and daughters of the kingdom. It is how we enter into holiness. It is everything that defines our existence. The difference between heaven and earth is defined by a boundary. The difference between born-again or not born-again is a boundary. Transition is measured in the boundaries we cross. We were there; now we are here.

Citizenship According to the Kingdom

As citizens of the kingdom, we pass easily across boundaries. We are in this world but not of it. By granting us access, we bring the message of kingdom to a lost and suffering world. Like Ambassadors bearing diplomatic passports, we navigate the world in spirit and in truth, aiming toward the goal for the prize of the upward call of God in Christ Jesus.

7

Passport

And in Your book were written
All the days that were ordained for me.

Psalm 139:16

THE PURPOSE OF GOD is the restoration of the Kingdom of God through the rights and responsibilities of citizenship.

The passport of the United States of America is a beautiful thing. Dark blue, compact, and representing the most powerful nation in the world, it opens many doors. It also describes us in sufficient detail so that any agency will know who they are admitting into their country. It tells us that in case of emergency, we are to notify the nearest American embassy or consulate or the State Department. In other words, if you get into a crisis, you need to contact your country through the U.S. embassies throughout the world. Why? Because your home country has the ability to either extract you from that hostile situation, translate you wherever they need you to go, or send help to secure you. A passport also states this information in several other languages so that if someone outside our country finds our passport, they know how to treat it. Those are the standards that our government applies to outsiders, telling them how they have to treat us or there will be consequences.

It is unlawful for any person other than the original, lawful recipient to use a passport. We can't give anybody our passport and allow them entry into the sphere of influence that we've been called to.

Finally, we read:

> U.S. government property. This passport is a property of the United States title 22 code of the Federal Regulation Section 51.9. It must be surrendered upon demand. Made by the authorized representative of the United States government.

I feel a weight on those words. As a U.S. citizen, if the government demanded my passport, I'd have to surrender it, which immobilizes me by restricting my travel beyond these United States. I also lose my passport if I commit a felony. Destruction of a passport should be reported immediately to local police authorities and the Passport Service, CLASP Unit, Washington, DC. We need to let the home country know if it is damaged, lost, or stolen.

There are many principles here that apply to the Kingdom of God. Let's start with Jesus' words in the gospel of John.

The thief comes only to steal and kill and destroy.

John 10:10

When we find ourselves in a situation where our authority's been damaged, stolen, or lost, and our legal ability to move around in another governmental structure is hampered, we need to call the home country and say, "My passport's been damaged. My ability to maneuver is restricted because of this. I need a reissuance of my passport, please."

Joan and I have had numerous passports. They contain stamps which identify the other nations we have visited. As a Philippine native, other nations have given Joan access because of her U.S. passport. Joan also has a Filipino passport, which allows her into countries that the U.S. passport won't allow her to enter.

So, our citizenship in a country gives us legal standing to do kingdom business in territories that do not yet belong to our king.

Passport

GOVERNMENTAL COVENANT

Citizenship is a governmental covenant between the individual and the issuing country. It applies to all citizens, regardless of race, color or creed. I may be white, but that doesn't mean I'm an American. In the Philippines, they look at white people and say, "You're white; you must be an American." But America contains a variety of races. Citizenship cannot be determined by the color of the skin, the pointedness of the nose, or the shape of the eyes. It doesn't work that way.

How do we determine citizenship? By the passport, the governmental documentation signifying an allegiance to a country. Citizenship grants certain rights and responsibilities. So, in a sense, the passport determines what authority I have. As a U.S. citizen, I have certain inalienable rights. Even when I'm in another country, I have rights. If I go to the U.S. embassy, I don't have to demand my rights. I can just invoke them. They have to let me through the door. If all hell is breaking loose on the outside and I come up to the gate and say, "I am an American citizen, open the gate." They won't say, "Greg, it is too hostile out there. Come back in an hour…if you can still walk." No, they'll open the gate. They may crack it a bit. I may have to squeeze past a surly Marine guard staring at the hostile crowd, but I'll get in. They'll even send the marines outside the gate to make sure I get through safely.

ANGELS, GOD'S MARINES

God sends his marines to help us in hostile situations. They are called angels. We need to learn to recognize and work with angels. Angels are sent to minister with us and to minister for us. The author of Hebrews told us:

> *Are they not all ministering spirits, sent out to provide service for the sake of those who will inherit salvation?*
>
> Hebrews 1:14

The Bible is full of angelic encounters. Gabriel came to Mary and told her she would bear God's son. Holy Spirit overshadowed her and the word was made flesh. An angel appeared to Jesus in the garden to refresh and strengthen him after he had endured the temptations with the devil. An angel appeared to Peter while he was in jail. That angel slapped him on the shoulder and said, "Wake up, man, I am opening doors for you. Get out of here." Remarkably, Peter was at peace in that jail cell despite knowing the next day he would be executed. He was satisfied and confident in his citizenship.

One of the most remarkable encounters with angels was when Daniel had been praying and fasting for 21 days, and an angel appeared before him. Here is what Daniel saw:

> *I raised my eyes and looked, and behold, there was a man dressed in linen, whose waist had a belt of pure gold of Uphaz. His body also was like topaz, his face had the appearance of lightning, his eyes were like flaming torches, his arms and feet like the gleam of polished bronze, and the sound of his words like the sound of a multitude.*
>
> Daniel 10:5-6

To summarize, this creature had pure gold radiating against linen, a face like lightening, flaming torches for arms, feet like brass and a voice thundering like a thousand people. No wonder Daniel fell to the ground like a dead man. Keeping in mind that angels can appear any way they choose, the angel's words to Daniel were borderline comical. Getting the trembling man to his feet, the angel said, "Fear not."

Fear not? Really? You show up looking like the finale to a heavy metal rock concert, and I'm supposed to "Fear not"?

Yeah...we need to learn to work with angels, even those with a twisted sense of humor.

Passport

CITIZENSHIP IS ACCESS TO RIGHTS

Citizenship requires a commitment to common law, ideals and values. This is one reason that our nation is in an uproar. Some of the people we've elected and sent to DC are from cultures outside America. They've come into this nation for one reason—to destroy our nation from within. They know they can't attack us from the outside. So, they come in, try to look like one of us, get elected to high positions, and set about changing the laws and culture in ways that weaken our country.

> *We have been so lazy and ethereally-focused that we are giving away this great nation through neglect.*

Daniel 7 refers to this. The enemy came in, wore out the saints, then tried to change the laws that govern the nations. The United States of America is not a democracy. A democracy is ruled by the majority. We are not ruled by the majority. We are a Constitutional Republic. A republic is a nation governed by law. It doesn't matter what the majority says about a particular topic; it matters what our law says.

Americans in general—and Christians in particular—have been so lazy and ethereally-focused that we are giving away this great nation through neglect. God has called this nation to take the gospel of the kingdom around the world, and we've given it over to people who don't know or respect our culture. Their goal is to change our culture.

There are parts of Minneapolis, Minnesota, where the police can't enter. Islam has taken over neighborhoods. Local people are enforcing Sharia law and have even fenced off these areas from the surrounding communities.

New York City has seen the rise of Chinese police stations enforcing pseudo laws on the local Chinese population. Some people tried that in Texas. It didn't go so well. Texas is different. Thank God for Texas.

> *Thank God for Texas.*

The United States does not operate by Sharia law. It does not operate by Chinese law. We operate by a system called the Constitution of the United States of America. The Constitution structures our rights and responsibilities. We are government ruled and governed by law, not by the rule of the majority. We need to understand that the loudest voice is not always the right voice. The most discontent people should not get their way by virtue of their bellicose antics.

We are faced with the tyranny of the minority. A few people got prayer removed from public school. Another minority brought abortion into our culture. A few have legalized homosexual marriage, which is remarkable given the small percentage of our nation that is homosexual. How have they done it? They supported certain candidates. They ran for office. They got elected. They wrote new laws. The same is happening with transgenderism. People in government are taking away the rights of parents to raise their children in the gender God gave them. They're proposing to put people in jail for telling a boy he's a boy when he thinks he's a girl.

The world has taken the wonderful characteristics of male and female and perverted them, making them ugly. It has pulled them out of covenant with God and instead created their own genders. We used to have laws protecting parents, children and prayer. Today, we have laws attacking these things.

Certainly, some laws need to stay; others need to go. The law is a living thing. It has to adapt with the times. In my hometown, if you tie your horse on the wrong hitching post, you can get a ticket. I haven't seen a horse in town in a long time, nor a hitching post either. But the law is still on the books. And so, it is still valid. Why? Because we are a nation governed by laws. Glory to God.

Passport

CITIZENSHIP IS A PRIVILEGE, NOT A RIGHT

There is a reason why it takes a legal immigrant a long time to get their citizenship in America. Becoming a citizen gives people rights and responsibilities that they don't know how to handle. As a citizen, they can influence the nation. They have a voice; they have a vote. They have the right to change things.

There are many people in our nation today who have come here illegally and are now demanding citizenship. Citizenship is a privilege, not a right. It's not something a person can demand. There is a legal process required, a vetting process, and it requires an oath of allegiance to the United States of America.

Joan was a green card holder for seven years before she could even apply for full citizenship. She had to fill out paperwork, submit to a background check, pay money, study the Constitution and know the Presidents. She had to know who her federal senators and congress people were. She had to recite the pledge of allegiance. She had to learn the national anthem—she didn't have to sing it, although that would have been beautiful—and learn the national motto: *E Pluribus Unum*—In God, We Trust. (All others pay cash.) Finally, she had to pass a test on all these things to qualify for citizenship.

Christians have a similar process. We have to qualify to be citizens of the Kingdom of God. Everybody doesn't get to be a citizen. Just because we are in God's world doesn't mean we belong to God. *Aren't we all God's children?* No, we are not all God's children. We are all God's creation, but we are not all God's children. There are qualifications to becoming his child.

You can't be Buddhist and be part of the Kingdom of God. You are disqualified; Buddhism is another kingdom. Likewise, you cannot be Muslim and be a part of the Kingdom of God. That's illegal. It's like people today running across our border and demanding citizenship. *Aren't we all going to get to heaven? Don't we serve the same God?* No, we are not all going to heaven. No, we do not serve the same God.

Allah is not Jehovah, even though Muslims have taken much of the Old Testament and put it into their Quran. They don't believe that Jesus is God. They believe he was a prophet, that he was a good man, and they adhere to some of the things he taught. Yet even though the Quran quotes Isaiah 9, which says Jesus is God, Muslims don't believe that he's God.

> And the government shall be upon his shoulders. And he shall be called, wonderful, counselor, mighty God, an everlasting Father.

That's in your Quran, we tell them. Your holy book is talking about Jesus. It blows their minds. Yet we don't serve the same God. They think Allah is God. He's not. And that makes all the difference. Our perception of reality is not a matter of logic. It's a matter of spirit. Our spiritual content determines what we accept as truth. This is why John told us:

> Beloved, do not believe every spirit, but test the spirits to see whether they are from God,
>
> 1 John 4:1

Denominationalism is another force in society that cannot give us access to the Kingdom. A lot of non-born-again people are embedded in churches. That is serious business. They've been recruited into a religion, but they've never been naturalized into the Kingdom.

Jesus was rough on religious people.

> Woe to you, scribes and Pharisees, hypocrites, because you travel around on sea and land to make one proselyte; and when he becomes one, you make him twice as much a son of hell as yourselves.
>
> Matthew 23:15

I think that's why God invented cussing, so he could deal with religion.

Passport

GOSPEL OF THE KINGDOM

We are told to preach the gospel, yet we need to understand what that means. If we preach the gospel of deliverance, does that mean we are preaching the gospel of the Kingdom? If we preach the gospel of healing, does that mean we are preaching the gospel of the Kingdom? Gospel simply means "good news." There's good news in deliverance. There's good news in healing. But it's not the good news we were told to preach. Those are manifestations of the good news.

> *Our responsibility as kingdom citizens is to bring people into the government of the Kingdom of God*

If we preach the gospel of salvation, surely, we are we preaching the gospel of the Kingdom, right? Isn't the gospel of the kingdom all about salvation? No, it's not. We are still preaching manifestations—the things that will happen once a person is in the kingdom.

Our responsibility as kingdom citizens is not to bring people into a religious experience. We are not trying to get them conformed to our religion. We are to bring them into the government of the Kingdom of God. We do this through our constitution: the Bible.

A friend of mine who was a part of a particular denomination for most of his life out of Cleveland, Tennessee, told me that they follow the Bible and their church's manual. Funny thing, though. Their manual supersedes the Bible. You must go through your manual to interpret the Bible. *Something's wrong there, Bill. Let's check our manual and figure out what it is.*

What religion promotes as the born-again experience ends up not being the born-again experience at all. A lot of people are in trouble, thinking they are on the road to God, and instead, they are being detoured to tradition. We have a lot of work to do. It's very troubling to me, heartbreaking in fact, because we just blanket over the core dysfunction. *Oh, they're in a steepled stained glass building or a shopping mall that has the name of a church over it. They're good. At least they're going to heaven.* I believe many of them are truly born-again, but what is being propagated through those pulpits is not bringing the salvation Jesus meant when he said, "You must be born-again."

At eight years old, I gave my life to Jesus. Of that, I have no doubt. I also have no doubt that I didn't have the power to sustain that relationship with Jesus, because when I was a teenager, I strayed way off the reservation.

So, what do we do to get people truly saved, and to keep them saved? Do we get them to pray a prayer? Give them false hope that their name is written in a book in heaven? Actually, when we get saved, the scripture doesn't say our name is written in the Book of Life. It says our name won't be scratched out of the Book of Life.

> *The one who conquers will be clothed thus in white garments, and I [Jesus] will never blot his name out of the book of life.*
>
> Revelation 3:5
>
> *May they be wiped out of the book of life, And may they not be recorded with the righteous.*
>
> Psalm 69:28

So, salvation is not a matter of adding to the book of life; it is a matter of not being removed from it.

If we are called to preach the gospel of the kingdom—and we are—it's vital that we understand what we are preaching. Key to this is knowing the deeper inferences to our citizenship.

Nobody can convince me that I'm not an American. Nobody can talk me out of my rights and responsibilities. In like manner, there needs to be that type of knowing in someone's life that they're born-again as a son or a daughter of God. I've given altar calls all over the world, and I can tell you that many people come up for the third, fourth, fifth, sixth and seventh time wanting to give their lives to Jesus. They want a relationship with him. But so far, all they've been given was a prayer. They have no power, no ability to transform, to adjust, to switch their citizenship from the world to the Kingdom of God. They said the prayer and went right back into the same world they were living in before they prayed.

Were they saved? I don't know. But I know they're not going to come into their God-given purpose without something more than a tearful altar call amidst forty-seven choruses of "Just As I Am." They're not being equipped to live out their new identity in a hostile nation.

> *Salvation is not a matter of adding to the book of life; it is a matter of not being removed from it.*

It's easy to get born-again. You say "Jesus, I believe in your cause and your purpose; I'm signing up for that. My allegiance is to you, Jesus. You loved me enough to die for me so I could get back into what you originally had for me. I accept that fact and I sell out to you."

Did I say easy? No, it's not easy. It's simple. It's profound. It's easy to get into, but it takes work to cultivate the commitment we make.

It's like saying "Yes" to a beautiful woman or a handsome man at your side, both of you dressed like 5th Avenue mannequins. A preacher stands in front. Bridesmaids and groomsmen make eyes at each other while they're supposed to be supporting the young couple who, at this moment, are scared spitless. A couple of I do's, and WHAM! Life changes forever. Simple.

When we are truly born-again—when we truly sell out—everything changes. Still, there's a lot to learn. Some things we work out, other things we walk out. We learn just like everyone who has gone before us. Even today, those of us who have been saved for over 40 years are still working out our own salvation with fear and trembling.

> *So then, my beloved, just as you have always obeyed, not as in my presence only, but now much more in my absence, work out your own salvation with fear and trembling;*
>
> Philippians 2:12

Nothing wrong with fear and trembling as long as we are focused on the right things.

Being a citizen of the kingdom is not a right we get just because we go to a church. Some denominations teach that if you come to this church, and you do this particular thing, then you are saved. Here's the catch: If you switch to another church, now you aren't saved. Some churches tell you that if you are not baptized exactly as they instruct, you are not saved. You can't go to heaven.

Well, being saved doesn't have much to do with going to heaven. It has to do with our lives being restored back into the original intent of God. The Church of Christ, from my earlier example, tells people they are not saved until they are baptized in their church. So, it is water baptism that saves you, not faith through grace. Good thing they have a manual that supersedes the Bible. Gets all those pesky scriptures out of the way of their man-made "truth."

Being saved doesn't have much to do with going to heaven. It has to do with our lives being restored back into the original intent of God.

Religion is leading people astray, and that's dangerous. Worse, it separates us from our creator God, who is a phenomenal God. He is a loving, gracious God who will go to great lengths to introduce himself to people. Some folks run from God their entire lives and come to one stunning conclusion: You can't run from God. Just ask that guy named Jonah. Three days of whale vomit and rotting fish, and he reached the same remarkable conclusion.

Jesus will even come to people on their deathbeds. I know a man who was once the prime minister of Ethiopia. This man's name is Tamrat Layne. He's a friend of mine and has written endorsements in our books.

He was thrown in prison for seven years and Jesus appeared to him seven times. Before his imprisonment, he was outspoken about his belief that there is no God. He was a communist and an atheist...until

Jesus walked into his cell and introduced himself. "This is me; would you like to receive me? I want to be your Lord."

True to his beliefs, Tamrat said, "No, I don't believe in you. You can go."

Well, Jesus came back to his cell five more times. Tamrat rejected him each time, saying, "I don't want anything to do with you."

The seventh time Jesus walked in, Tamrat was ready. He gave his life to Jesus and was born-again. He remembers the day and hour that this happened. Amazingly, at the same hour, Jesus appeared to Tamrat's wife in their house. She was born-again and filled with the Holy Spirit. Within a few months, Tamrat was released from prison to join his wife and children. The U.S. government allowed him to emigrate so he could escape further persecution. God is so faithful.

> *Where can I go from Your Spirit?*
> *Or where can I flee from Your presence?*
> *If I ascend to heaven, You are there;*
> *If I make my bed in Sheol, behold, You are there.*
> *If I take up the wings of the dawn,*
> *If I dwell in the remotest part of the sea,*
> *Even there Your hand will lead me,*
> *And Your right hand will take hold of me..*
>
> Psalm 139:7-10

More people are going to heaven than we think. As we discussed, getting saved is about more than getting to heaven. It's about fulfilling God's call on our lives. Therein lies the rub. Many of those experiencing last minute salvations are not going to be able to walk out their God-given purpose. Part of our assignment, as citizens of the kingdom, is to introduce them to the King who brings them back into power to realize their original intent and design. We need people of purpose to restore the earth. We need people walking out their destiny to take back what Adam gave away. Jesus empowered us to do that. To fulfill that mandate, however, we have to do more than make converts. Jesus never told us to make converts. He told us to make disciples.

> *Go, therefore, and make disciples of all the nations, baptizing them in the name of the Father and the Son and the Holy Spirit….*
>
> Mathew 28:19

Converts might make heaven, but disciples make history. Sometimes they even upset the world.

> *When they did not find them, they began dragging Jason and some brothers before the city authorities, shouting, "These men who have upset the world have come here also."*
>
> Acts 17:6

> *Converts might make heaven, but disciples make history. Sometimes they even upset the world.*

Society is full of world-turner-upside-downers. They just don't know which side they're really on. The people carrying signs, shutting down highways, screaming at congressional hearings, mutilating their bodies and encouraging others to do the same…these are passionate world changers. They're just misguided—even deceived—world-changers. The richest soil grows the tallest weeds.

We need to saturate the world with the Kingdom of God, raising the consciousness of the evil of religion. We need a passion to go after those that don't know Jesus as King and bring them into the kingdom. We can't just say, "Well, the Lord will take care of it; he'll sort them out." No, we have a responsibility to get the family back.

> *And He said to them, "Go into all the world and preach the gospel to all creation. The one who has believed and has been baptized will be saved; but the one who has not believed will be condemned."*
>
> Mark 16:15-16

They're not totally lost; they're still family—the human family. Their names are in the Book of Life. Salvation ensures that their names will not be scratched out when they pass. Interestingly, what the Bible calls *the lost* is not the people of earth, but the Kingdom of God on the earth.

> *For the Son of Man has come to seek and to save that which was lost,*
>
> Luke 19:10

Jesus came to seek and to save *that which was lost,* not *those who were lost*. We are restoring the kingdom so that mankind can be restored.

CITIZENSHIP AS A CONSTITUTIONAL CONTRACT

Citizenship defines the constitutional contract between the state and the individual. If you are an American citizen, you have a contract with America. We, the people, created it. Our citizenship is based solely on that contract, which is the Constitution. It's not based on anything else. We have no rights beyond the structure of our Constitution. The Constitution is the power of citizenship.

Jesus came to seek and to save that which was lost, not those who were lost.

The constitutional contract in the Kingdom of God is the Bible. Our confidence in our legal standing is from our understanding of this governing document. It defines the boundaries of our citizenship.

Long ago, two people decided they wanted the knowledge of good and evil. Only, they didn't do it God's way. In a sense, what we have in scripture is an answer to their desire. The Bible clearly tells us what is good and what is evil, what brings us to life and what consigns us to death. Yet it does so in a way that we can handle it. It puts new wine in new wineskins. Regarding our citizenship rights and responsibilities, if we can find it in scripture, we have the right to it. Amen!

Of course, there are people who want to add different books to the Bible. The Catholic Bible adds the Apocrypha—12 books that Protestants don't recognize. There are also many gospels beyond the big four. The key is this: *Tread carefully*. With regard books like Maccabees I, Mac-the-Bees II, Mac-and-Cheese III, and Whatahangover IV, non-canonized books can be a source of information, but only in the hands of Holy Spirit.

CITIZENSHIP IS THE LEGAL STATUS

Citizenship in the kingdom is the legal status of the individual in relationship with the constitution, guaranteeing all rights and privileges afforded therein. Citizenship is our legal status. It is based on what is delineated in scripture.

Those who fear those rights—who fear the empowerment of God's people that arises from knowing those rights—will try to remove them. The good news is: God's written word can't be altered. It's indelible. Sure, people can burn the pages, but they miss the point. God's word is eternal. Further, it surrounds us. Just as you can't outrun God, you can't avoid his word. You need to be higher than the one who wrote it before you can change it. And there isn't anyone who fits that description. When God introduced himself to Moses, he called himself "I am," because there was no one higher. He's the source. The absolute.

The power of citizenship comes from our relationship to the Constitution. The same principle applies to the Kingdom of God. How we relate to the constitution—the Bible—is what guarantees us all that is written herein. This gives us legal rights. Those rights are not

> *When God introduced himself to Moses, he called himself "I am," because there was no one higher. He's the source. The absolute.*

based on how we feel. They are not based on whether or not we are prayed up. They are based on one thing: "It is written...."

The constitutionally protected status of the individual with respect to the state is protected and guaranteed by law. Now it doesn't mean the state of the land, but our state as a citizen. My standing as a citizen is guaranteed. I'm constitutionally protected.

CITIZENSHIP IS THE CONFERENCE OF A NATION

Citizenship is the conference of a nation on the individual. It is the gathering. It can be Congress, the Congress of, the whole of the sum of, the nation in an individual. Citizenship is the sum of America in you. America as a citizen, America is summed up in me. Now, I may not always know how to partake of it. I may not always invoke what it means, but it is summed up in me as a citizen. Which means citizens embody everything in the Constitution, including the Bill of Rights and the rest of the amendments.

America is a nation of the people, for the people, by the people. We embody the nation. The nation is not the nation without the people. The constitution is not the constitution without the embodiment of the people. It's the same regarding the kingdom of God.

Ephesians says that all things are summed up in Christ Jesus.

> *He made known to us the mystery of His will, according to His good pleasure which He set forth in Him, regarding His plan of the fullness of the times, to bring all things together in Christ, things in the heavens and things on the earth.*
>
> Ephesians 1:9-10

Our citizenship in the kingdom is embodied in Christ. The word *embodied* tells us that Jesus is the godhead bodily. The Kingdom of God is summed up in Christ Jesus,

> *For in Him all the fullness of Deity dwells in bodily form.*
>
> Colossians 2:9

> *The Kingdom of God is not somewhere we go. The Kingdom of God is everywhere we go.*

I get my citizenship by being in him and him in me. My citizenship in the Kingdom of God is not because I prayed a prayer, or I go to church, or I give my money, or I do everything right. My citizenship is in Christ Jesus. I am in him, and all things are summed up in him. Therefore, he embodies the sum total of our Constitution. He fulfilled everything. He is the sum of all that heaven has. And as I am in him, he is in me. Therefore, if he embodies it all, I embody it all, because I'm in him. If I'm outside of him, and I'm going through religious rituals and ordinances, I don't embody the Kingdom of God. I have a form of godliness but no power. I'm his representative as ambassador in the earth, and everything I do, I do through him, not through myself alone.

We need to understand that we are not weak, worthless vessels that need Jesus to make it through the day. When we step into him, we become empowered sons and daughters. We can now step into the dominion of the sphere of influence that God has given us in which to rule and reign. When people see us, they see Christ.

CITIZENSHIP IN A COUNTRY

We can't be a member of America. We have to become a Citizen. Citizenship is the receiving of a country. When we were born-again, we become citizens of the Kingdom of God. As such, we didn't just receive Jesus; we received a nation. All of the power of the country is at our disposal in our assignments as ambassadors.

Passport

- Religion says we have Jesus….and we do. But kingdom says more: We have a nation.
- Religion says we have Jesus as a savior. But Kingdom says we have a country with a king, and Jesus is that king.
- Religion reduces Jesus to merely a savior. Kingdom releases Jesus into our lives as a King.

Citizenship is the receiving of a nation, a country, a kingdom. Let the power of that truth sink in. Whenever we become a naturalized United States citizen, we don't just get a passport. We don't just get something that helps us travel easier. We receive the entirety of the nation. A citizen embodies the Constitution. We don't just embody the right to vote. We embody the entirety of this nation as one born in another nation.

"Repent for the Kingdom of God is at hand" literally means "repent for the Kingdom of God is near. We know that the Kingdom of God is within us. Therefore, the Kingdom of God is not somewhere we go. The Kingdom of God is everywhere we go.

8
Uniqueness of Kingdom Citizenship

THERE ARE ASPECTS of the Kingdom of God that set it apart from the concepts of membership or servitude. God's kingdom is a unique environment from which we are commanded to go forth and restore the earth. Here are some of its remarkable qualities.

<u>All citizens are related to the king.</u>

In the Kingdom of God, we don't have any cousins. No kissing cousins, no cousins twice-removed on our mother's side. Neither do we have any crazy uncles telling us stories from the War of 1812. We don't have any aunties reeking of stale perfume and crushing us with hugs at Christmas dinner. We are all sons and daughters; we are all brothers and sisters. The kingdom has one bloodline, not many bloodlines. We all share a direct bloodline to the king, a bloodline that started with Jesus.

<u>All citizens have access to government authority.</u>

As citizens, we rule and reign with Jesus right now in heavenly places. Even though you might be reading this in your favorite armchair, a gentle fire crackling under the hearth, a warm cat purring in your lap, you are legally seated in heaven with Jesus. In this position, we have access to government authority; indeed, we embody it. Why? Because we rule from thrones.

> *But God, being rich in mercy, because of His great love with which He loved us, even when we were dead in our wrongdoings, made us alive together with Christ (by grace you have been saved), and raised us up with Him, and seated us with Him in the heavenly places in Christ Jesus, so that in the ages to come He might show the boundless riches of His grace in kindness toward us in Christ Jesus.*
>
> Ephesians 2:4-7

All citizens are appointed ambassadors.

Recall our frequent reference to rights and responsibilities. Everybody wants their rights. (Who doesn't?) Yet not all are ready to accept their responsibilities. Well...just hanging on 'til heaven ain't gonna cut it. All who are in the kingdom, all who have had authority conferred upon them, are ambassadors in connection with God's assignment for their lives. This is why we all have the authority. It is to represent and expand the Kingdom of God in the spheres of influence that God has assigned us to.

The attitude of, "Well, I'm just going to live my life and go to heaven," reflects poor stewardship of our governmental standing. We are always on a diplomatic assignment. No matter where an ambassador goes, they are always an ambassador. They carry their home nation everywhere. Thus, they are always accountable for their actions.

The Kingdom of God has standards, morals and culture that ambassadors are expected to embody. Ambassadors don't go to foreign nations and assimilate into that nation. There's a saying in the foreign service: "You go native; you go home." The uniqueness of the citizenship in the kingdom is that all of us have governmental authority. We are prepared for service, and to service we shall go.

At a fundamental level, our service is to represent Christ (preferably in a favorable light). People look at us and expect to see Christ and the kingdom. Do they? Our actions are the determinant.

<u>All citizens are rulers and leaders in the nation.</u>

In the Kingdom of God, each of us is a leader. Just as our ambassadorship is indelible, no one gets to avoid being a leader. Why? Because God has given all of us a sphere of influence, a place of responsibility. We are not on this earth to blend in, not totally. We are here to influence, to change, to lead. Leaders are not called to be just like everyone else. That's belonging; it's not leading. Leaders are different just as the lead sled dog is different. Here's the good news: Unless you are the lead dog, the view never changes.

Leadership starts with our own lives. We must govern ourselves well. From there, we should govern our families, our workplaces, communities and regions. Leadership is a kingdom culture value.

Leadership starts with our own lives. We must govern ourselves well.

As members of our nation, we are to participate in government within our realm of influence. In addition, there are specific spheres of influence that God gives us to function in as ambassadors. Find those areas, get connected, and be willing to stand out. Remember: sheep don't lead sheep.

<u>All citizens have commonwealth status.</u>

Some states in the U.S. are commonwealths. For example, Virginia is called the Commonwealth of Virginia. Also, some nations that once were connected to Great Britain are now called Commonwealths. These countries are ruled independently—each has their own governmental structures. Australia, even though it's an independent nation now, started out as a prison colony for Great Britain. It was a brutal environment. From its fatal shores, God raised up a nation for his purpose. It was under the rule of Great Britain for many years, and is still considered under the crown because it is a commonwealth. (But don't tell the Aussies that when they play the bloody poms at cricket.) Canada is also an independent nation but still considered a commonwealth to Great Britain.

In a commonwealth, as the name implies, everyone shares the wealth, status and lifestyle of the crown—the king or queen of Great Britain.

In the Kingdom of God, we all share a commonwealth. The wealth involves more than money. We share status, standing, influence and other resources. It is a common bond that can be called upon when needed.

<u>All kingdom citizens are from one family.</u>

In God's kingdom, we are all related to the King, but do we realize the extent of it? In our society today, people can be related through one father but have different mothers. It's not that way in the kingdom. We are not stepbrothers and stepsisters. We are all from one source. That is what *father* means: *source*. We are from one family. There is no status of familial relationship. Everyone has a seat at the table, everyone has a package under the tree. No one is better than the other. No one is left out. Welcome to the family.

<u>Citizenship empowers us for the now.</u>

The rights and responsibilities of citizenship in the kingdom do not manifest in the future. Citizenship empowers us for the present. Consider: We don't have to wait to partake of the rights and responsibilities of the United States Constitution, do we? Nor do we have to wait to partake of the rights and responsibilities of the Kingdom of God. We were born into it; it is ours; now put your hand to the plow! It's childhood's end.

PRAYER IN THE KINGDOM

Prayer is different for kingdom citizens. It is the most unique aspect of being a kingdom citizen. It is vital to our function. Religion teaches prayer as wearing out two holes in the rug where we kneel beside our bed each night, hands folded, saying: "Now I lay me down to sleep. I pray my soul to keep."

That's the way I was raised. Prayer was either begging God to do something or trying to persuade God to do something. Sometimes it was just hollering for help. (Those were my favorite prayers—usually while gripping a steering wheel or fleeing the consequences of my latest mischief.)

Fortunately, prayer is more than these things. Prayer is actually petitioning in the sense of requesting what is within our legal rights to obtain. Prayer is a governmental term, not a religious term. Thus, it is not a religious activity but a governmental activity.

> *When properly understood, prayer results in us taking godly action without God's direct involvement.*

Prayer is two-way communication. It's not merely us clamoring at God, hurling our latest cares or desires in God's general direction. It works two ways: God hears from us; we hear from God. That's the nature of petitioning. It's letting God know what we need in a situation. But more so, it's us exercising the power and authority we have from God to obtain what we need.

When properly understood, prayer results in us taking godly action without God's direct involvement. Not exclusive of God, but in harmony with God. As we mature, we learn the ways of God; they become a part of our nature. In time, God doesn't have to tell us everything to do. We know what he wants, and we do it. Prayer is how we get it done.

KINGDOM PRINCIPLE OF PETITION

To understand the purpose and the power of prayer, we must understand the kingdom. When we bring prayer to the Kingdom of God, we see it through an entirely new lens.

As with most things, taking prayer out of the kingdom environment relegates it to a religious activity; a comfort, perhaps; a way to connect our fledgling faith with God's abundant provision. At worse, it becomes a religious busyness that rarely produces results.

We need to see prayer differently. Let's start here:

Therefore, when He comes into the world, He says,

> *"You have not desired sacrifice and offering,*
> *But You have prepared a body for Me;*
> *You have not taken pleasure in whole burnt offerings and offerings for sin.*
> *Then I said, 'Behold, I have come*
> *(It is written of Me in the scroll of the book)*
> *To do Your will, O God.'"*

Hebrews 10:5-7

Let's look at key passages of this scripture.

"Therefore, when He comes into the world...." This is a prophetic word about Jesus; it is from the Old Testament.

"Sacrifice and offering you did not desire...." That refers to religious activity.

"... but a body you have prepared for me...." This is the flesh and blood of Jesus.

"You have not taken pleasure in whole burnt offerings and offerings for sin." Refers to God's disdain for religion.

Surprising, isn't it? God takes no pleasure in burnt offerings and sacrifices for sin. Yet, isn't he the one who prescribed such practices in the first place? Yes, he is. But he didn't like it. The body prepared for the forgiveness of sins was Jesus, his son. I suspect God liked that even less, but he knew it had to be done.

"Then I said, 'Behold, I have come.'" This is Jesus. And how did he arrive?

"It is written of Me in the scroll of the book." What book? Not the Bible. It hadn't been compiled yet. He's talking about the Old Testament—the law and the prophets. He's also referring to the books that are in heaven—the books of destiny.

> *It is written of Me in the scroll of the book*
> *To do Your will, O God.*

Psalms 139 talks about books that God has written about each of us, things recorded in heaven. When people prophesy over us, they are reading from that book. They may not see a scroll; they may not see a book. But they're pulling from God's book--the things he wrote and desires about us. God prophesied over us before we ever showed up. It was recorded in heaven. Amen?

"It is written of me," said Jesus. Where? "In the scroll of the book." For what reason? "To do your will, O' God."

Jesus didn't come to do his own will. In the kingdom, you don't get to do your will unless it aligns with the king's will. Remarkably, God's will is pretty wide on most things. Who plants a garden and says "Green beans, you grow precisely as I dictate. Right here: up an inch, over 2 inches, and exactly 14.3 inches long." Sure, we tend our gardens, but we do so in the sense of boundaries. It's more like, "Green beans: here's soil, water, sunlight and a pole to climb. Have at it. Supper's at 6."

I AM SOME BODY

Our physical body is the most important part of our existence on the earth. People often say, "Wait. Is not my spirit the most important part?" Sadly, these people do not read my books. If they did, they would understand that it is not their spirit, but their body, that is the most important. Here's why.

Let's begin with a few statements about prayer and petition and the physical body. As I said earlier, most people don't know how to pray from a kingdom mindset. And yet, prayer is a vital kingdom activity on earth. Remember, prayer is petitioning. Prayer is going back to the home country, to the throne, and petitioning things from the unseen realm into the seen realm. Prayer is not begging God. He's already given you what you need. You are a citizen. You have rights. You have standing. Now stand on your rights as a citizen!

Prayer is actually a legal term used in legal briefs and courtrooms. In the kingdom, prayer is accessing the throne room of God to petition him for things that we need, getting his thoughts, guidance and will on things. This is in stark contrast to reacting to things. Effective prayer is proactive. It comes from knowing our place, operating from our rights, and knowing that it's not our urgency that moves God as much as it is our faith in where we stand with God. That place is the throne room. Prayer is praying about building a new dam long before the river floods, the crops are wiped out, and you watch everything you've built over a lifetime get swept into the Gulf of Mexico.

> *Prayer is standing on our own two feet. We know what the King wants. We don't always have to ask him.*

Prayer is standing on our own two feet as redeemed men and women—as sons and daughters of the kingdom. We know what the King wants. We don't always have to ask him. We know what his will is in certain situations. We don't have to keep running back every time, reinventing our theology to fit the present circumstance. Not only do we hear his heart on matters; we also share his heart. The things of God are growing in us.

> *I was made a minister of this church according to the commission from God granted to me for your benefit, so that I might fully carry out the preaching of the word of God, that is, the mystery which had been hidden from the past ages and generations, but now has been revealed to His saints, to whom God willed to make known what the wealth*

of the glory of this mystery among the Gentiles is, <u>the mystery that is Christ in you, the hope of glory.</u>

Colossians 1;25-27

We know it is God's will to heal people. We know it is his will that all should be saved and not perish. How do we know? Because it has become our will as well, and we flow with him. We don't have to pray to understand it's his will. We don't even have to pray for God to intervene because we embody the entire nation. Remember adoption: it is when God says: "When you see him or her, you see me."

Jesus told us to lay hands on the sick and they will be healed. So, we don't have to pray, "God, would you please heal this person?" God says, "You heal him."

Religion says we are not healers. Kingdom says we are healers because we embody the kingdom. If Christ is in each of us, and he is our hope of glory—the weightiness of the presence of God—then our body is the most important thing we have in this earth. Healing flows through it; dominion flows; deliverance flows. This is why Jesus came to earth in a body. And not just any body. He came as Jesus: unique fingerprints, DNA, even voice print.

PARTNERING WITH GOD

Prayer is an ambassador's number one responsibility. John Wesley understood something about prayer that few people understand.

"Without God, we cannot; without us, God will not."

Praying is partnering with God in the living of our lives.

John Wesley

The fact is, God needs us. This is how God set things up here on earth. Man can do nothing without God. Yet there is also another reality. On earth, God will do nothing without man.

There's an old saying: If the devil wants to do something on earth, he gets a man to do it. God does nothing on earth without a human;

neither does the devil. Both understand the laws of human involvement. This is why the serpent had to tempt Eve rather than outright taking what he wanted.

> *Our body is the most important thing we have in this earth. Healing flows. Dominion flows. Deliverance flows.*

Because of how God established the order of our earthly existence, a partnership between heaven and earth is required for things to happen on the earth. This means that what happens on the earth depends on us.

Religion blames God for what happens on earth. The argument is based on God's sovereignty. *Well, if this is happening in the earth, then it must be God's will, because God controls everything.* Quite the contrary, God does not control everything. What is happening could be the opposite of God's will. It could be happening because men are not walking in relationship with God. Therefore, men are aligned with what the enemy is doing in the earth.

- Abortion is not God's fault. It's man's fault.
- Murder is not God's fault. It's man's fault.
- Human trafficking is not God's fault. It's man's fault.
- A mean mother-in-law is not God's fault. Well....

God has no part in those things, so why are they happening on earth? It's because humans are allowing them to happen. We cannot say that these things are within the sovereignty of God if they are outside the nature of God. God doesn't sanction ungodly behavior.

Here's another excuse that Christians use...usually every four years. "Well, if this person is President, it must be the will of God." No. It's the will of the people. Because some Christians don't get up off their "do nothings" and go vote for the person that God wanted. *Well, if it's God's will....* Phooey! (Sorry. Have to keep this PG.) There have been prophetic words about certain people being president and leading our nation. Here's the problem. Prophetic words are conditional based on our participation. Prophetic words released in our lives are based on us partnering with heaven and walking in the direction the prophetic word leads us.

The prophetic words over a situation are not going to materialize without mature sons and daughters of God standing up, taking ownership of those prophetic words, partnering with God, and manifesting those words through men in the government—both the Kingdom of God and the law of the land. In that order.

I'm not saying God doesn't move sovereignly. There are times that God does move sovereignly, but it is not God's common practice to move sovereignly in the earth. He does that through men and women of the kingdom. Citizens...according to the kingdom.

Prayer definition

Prayer is not an option for the believer. Prayer is a necessity. Prayer is earthly permission for heavenly interference.

- We need to be people of petitioning.
- We need to stop praying, "God, move in my situation."
- We need to stop praying, "God, give me a breakthrough."
- We need to stop praying, "God, would you do something about my situation and help me?"

Instead, let's pray:

- Father, how do I partner with you to get out of this thing I'm in?
- Father, what do you need me to do to cause this situation to be rectified?
- Father, what is it that you want to do with me as your partner in the earth?
- Father, what is it that I need for breakthrough in my life?"

Many of us find ourselves in places where we want God to move supernaturally for us. But if he did that, we'd find ourselves right back in that same mess again. He wants a partnership with us. We are being trained to partner with him. Think of a child who continually breaks her toys, only to have her dad fix them. Finally, one day, the dad says "No." The child stares at her broken toys for days. Finally, she carries them to her dad and says, "Let's fix them." He smiles and takes her to his workshop.

We are called to partner with our Father. We have the tools. Let's learn to use them. Let's get to work.

9

Power of Humans

POWER IS EVERYTHING; so the saying goes. And it makes sense. Without power, nothing gets done. Power is the ability to do work. Horsepower is the work one horse can do. Manpower is the work one man can do. Miracle power is the work one mother with three kids, a job and an unfinished MBA can do.

Alfred Noble knew a thing or two about power. He was the engineer who invented dynamite. He had high hopes for its use in construction. *Think of the great things we can build with it.* He made a lot of money, but things didn't go as planned. People had other ideas. *Think of the things we can blow up with it.* In the end, he left a considerable portion of his fortune to the establishment of the Nobel prizes in Physics, Chemistry, Medicine, Literature and Peace. Apparently, power is not everything. Using it properly is also important. We call that authority.

Religion's solution to the misuse of power is to say Christians have no power. Yet we know that's not true. As citizens of the kingdom, we are full of power. The most powerful creature on the earth is you: the human.

What does our power look like? First of all, God only gave legal authority on the earth to humans.

> Then God said, "Let Us make mankind in Our image, according to Our likeness; and let them rule over the fish of the sea and over the birds of the sky and over the livestock and over all the earth, and over every crawling thing that crawls on the earth."
>
> Genesis 1:26

"We are going to make a man our likeness, then we are going to let them *radah* (rule) over the fish, the birds, the cattle, and all the creeps on the earth."

> So God created man in His own image, in the image of God He created him; male and female He created them.
>
> Genesis 1:27 NKJV

God rules with his words. God's decrees set things in motion. Talk about power! Now, when God said, "Be fruitful, multiply, fill the earth, subdue it, and *radah* over it," who did God say this to? Man. *Adamah*. Human beings.

And when did God say it? Right before he made humans. Humankind is *adamah*. We are the *Adamic* race. No matter your gender, color, ethnic origins, if you are a human, you are *Adamic*. As he created humans in that *Adamic* race, he created two models: male and female. (Not sixty-seven.) Henry Ford famously said you could get your car in any color you wanted...as long as it was black. God's a little more generous. *Here's your menu. Column A and column B. Oh, and I get to choose...not you.*

EVERYONE'S DIRT IS THE SAME

So, what is a human, anyway? Let's start here:

> Now may the God of peace Himself sanctify you entirely; and may your spirit and soul and body be kept complete, without blame at the coming of our Lord Jesus Christ.
>
> 1 Thessalonians 5:23

Power of Humans

The Apostle Paul prayed for God to sanctify us entirely. What is our entirety? Well, he lists it. According to Paul, we are spirit, soul and body. Our spirit is that part of us that functions in the unseen realm. It is our energy; our life force. When Jesus gave up his spirit on the cross, he died. "And Jesus cried out again with a loud voice and gave up His spirit" (Matthew 27:50).

> *We are the Adamic race. No matter your gender, color, ethnic origins, if you are a human, you are Adamic.*

Our bodies are also a necessary part of us. They are of dirt stuff. Scripture says,

Then the Lord God formed the man of dust from the ground, and breathed into his nostrils the breath of life; and the man became a living person.

Genesis 2:7

What did God form out of the dust? God formed the man. Notice that he was not making a body *for* the man; he was making the man himself. He was creating the physical aspect of our beings. Of course, our body responds to the spiritual dimension as well, else how could Jesus heal people with a word of faith? So, one part of our being is of spiritual substance, and another part is of physical substance.

This is why, when a person leaves their body, we dump it back in the dirt. Ashes to ashes, dust to dust.

A little boy learned that lesson in Sunday School one day. When he came home, he rushed to his bedroom, looked under his bed and called for his mom. "You better get in here quick," he said. "Somebody's either coming or going."

Racial prejudice breaks down when we realize that we are all dirt. Whether your dirt is black, white, red, yellow, brown, pink, purple, polka-dotted or tattooed, it's dirt. Beautiful, sensuous, mighty dirt. That is important to understand. Everyone's dirt is the same in humanity. Never judge someone's worth by the color of their dirt.

Turns out, however, that dirt is much more important to our function in the kingdom than most people think. We are told:

> *Or do you not know that your body is a temple of the Holy Spirit within you, whom you have from God, and that you are not your own? For you have been bought for a price: therefore glorify God in your body.*
>
> Corinthians 6: 19-20

We are to glorify God in our bodies. Why? Because they are temples of God's spirit. Let me explain how this works.

The Hebrew word for "dirt" is the word *humas*. The Hebrew word for "man" is the word *ish*. In Genesis 1:26, God was saying: "Let us make man, *ish*, in our image."

A human being is a mystery. We are spirit, soul, and body. When we say human, then, it is not simply a word to describe these bipeds walking around looking to see what they can blow up. We are an exquisite combination of heaven and earth, of supernatural and natural, of body and spirit, which we call...soul.

Look again at Genesis 2:7.

> *Then the Lord God formed the man of dust from the ground, and breathed into his nostrils the breath of life; and the man became a living person.*
>
> Genesis 2:7

God formed the man out of the ground. The ground was a part of the man. Yet the man was not alive until God "breathed into his nostrils the breath of life." He gave man spirit.

What happened when the body of the man came in contact with God's spirit of life? "...the man became a living person."

The King James actually says it better:

> *And the Lord God formed man of the dust of the ground, and breathed into his nostrils the breath of life; <u>and man became a living soul.</u>*
>
> Genesis 2:7 KJV

Here is a convenient way to think of it. Picture a candle surrounded by a stained-glass shade. With the candle unlit, the shade is dark, indistinct. But when we light the candle, the shade comes alive. It glows with the light of life from the candle.

> *Many things are illegal but they're still here. Why? Because the citizens of the kingdom have yet to fully rise up in power and dominion and declare the Kingdom of God throughout our earth.*

Now, imagine that the flame is God's Spirit of life. The stained-glass shade is the body. And the resultant image—the combination of spirit and body—forms our soul. Together: spirit, body, soul, we are human beings. Take one away—any one—and we are incomplete. We cannot function on the earth.

Jesus died when he gave up his spirit on the cross. Souls under the throne of God cried out for vengeance and were given white robes—a form of covering. These and others are examples of what happens when we are apart...literally. This is why the restoration of the earth—the new earth—includes the restoration of humans: body, soul and spirit. Our bodies are vital to our activity on earth.

People say that clothes make the man. I believe that's true. Naked people have very little influence in the world. What's more (or less, as the case may be), people without bodies have zero authority in the world, assuming we can discount a ghost or three that seem to cause a great deal of angst but little else.

We influence our world in many ways. Prayer is authorized humans—those with bodies, spirits and souls—accessing God's resources for the human race. When God gave man dominion over the earth, he was speaking to humans as spirit, soul and body. Therefore, the only being that has a legal right to govern the earth is a man with a spirit, soul and body. A human. Any spirit entity without a dirt body is illegal to rule (*radah*) on earth.

Until we understand this concept, the Bible will not make sense, including the incarnation of Jesus. Neither will spiritual warfare. Incarnation is from the word *carno*, which means "dirt" in the Hebrew. The word *carno* is in the word *incarnation,* meaning "spirit in dirt." God became a human. The incarnation of Christ meant that the Spirit of God entered a dirt body.

So, any person without a body is illegal on the earth. Jesus had to have a body to be legal in the earth. This is why we read in Hebrews 10:5:

> *"You have not desired sacrifice and offering,*
> *But you have prepared a body for Me;*

Of course, many things in this world are illegal but they're still here. Why? Because the citizens of the kingdom have yet to fully rise up in power and dominion and declare the Kingdom of God throughout our earth. Demons are illegal; they're still here...but not for long. Our most powerful weapon involves our body. It conveys our spiritual energy much like a rifle barrel conveys the energy of the gunpowder. We could even think of the soul as the bullet.

When we give up our spirit, we die. Depending on our cultural understanding, we call this death, or being with Jesus, or grandma's going to be in the ground for a while. In scripture, Paul depicts death as sleep, not something to be mourned but to be understood.

> *But we do not want you to be uninformed, brothers and sisters, about those who are asleep, so that you will not grieve as indeed the rest of mankind do, who have no hope. For if we believe that Jesus died and rose from the dead, so also God will bring with Him those who have fallen asleep through Jesus.*
>
> 1 Thessalonians 4:13-14

Our spiritual side never dies, so we never actually die. Speaking in general terms, Paul said that to be absent from the body is to be present with God.

Yes, we have confident and hopeful courage, and are pleased rather to be away from home, out of the body, and to be at home with the Lord.

2 Corinthians 5:8 AMPC

When we die, our body stops functioning. In a sense, we become illegal in the earth. We have no right to function here, so we have to leave.

This a powerful concept. Turned around, it says that our time to influence the earth is at hand. No time like the present. If you think you're going to die, go to heaven and make intercessions for the saints from your ethereal throne, think again. Jesus already has that job. The time—indeed, the opportunity—for humans to establish the kingdom of God is now.

The most powerful weapon we possess on this earth as an ambassador, as a son, as a daughter, as a citizen of the Kingdom of God, is our body. Think of it as your passport. If I am in the Philippines without a passport, I'm illegal. If I show up in Russia, stand in the middle of Red Square and declare: "People of Russia, I am here to lead you out of darkness," I better have a passport. Because if I don't, guess what? I'm illegal, and quite possibly quickly dead.

Our body is our passport to the earth; it makes us legal residents; it makes us citizens.

This is why demons try to enter people's bodies. They need legal rights on the earth to carry out their business. Demons aren't stupid. They know they're illegal without a body. Do we ever read of a demon arguing with Jesus? Even once? Begging...yes. But trying to gain the upper hand? The slightest whimper of defiance? Nope. Why? Because they know they're caught, exposed, and God's word is the absolute in heaven and on earth.

You believe that God is one. You do well; the demons also believe, and shudder.

James 2:19

Citizenship According to the Kingdom

> *Our body is our passport to the earth; it makes us legal residents; it makes us citizens.*

We are able to cast evil spirits out of people because they have no legal authority here. They're illegally trespassing in something that does not belong to them.

The fact is, God set it up this way, and while we can cheer that we have authority, Jesus' words should echo deep in our consciences.

Nevertheless, do not rejoice in this, that the spirits are subject to you, but rejoice that your names are recorded in heaven.

Luke 10:20

Yay! We are humans. We...are...some...body! We have power—our God-given authority. Sounds great, doesn't it? Yes, God is sovereign, but he's not inclined to do what he assigned—and equipped—man to do.

Recall Genesis 1:26. When God gave mankind dominion over the earth, he did not include himself. No matter how we try to parse the Hebrew, employ whatever study, concordance, or scripture-bending tool we can find, we cannot escape the fact that God removed himself from the immediate affairs of the earth and gave dominion to humans. When God said, "Let them have dominion over the earth," he was establishing a legal decree. See, when God speaks, everything he says becomes law. And while God is above the law—he made the law for a reason. He wants mankind to grow up.

Want to change the evil things in this world?

Humans have the authority on the earth.

Want to establish the Kingdom of God?

Humans have authority on the earth.

Want to stop rivers from flooding, children from starving, the devil from winning?

Humans have authority on the earth.
Want the Atlanta Braves to win the World Series?
Well, there's always God's sovereignty.

GOD IS SOVEREIGN

For the record, God occasionally does intervene into the affairs of man. Indeed, the earth still belongs to the Lord the way a landlord owns the property that he leases. We know this from Psalm 24.

> *The earth is the Lord's, and all it contains,*
> *The world, and those who live in it.*
> *For He has founded it upon the seas*
> *And established it upon the rivers.*
>
> Psalm 24:1-2

This is further reinforced by Isaiah:

> *I am God, and there is no other;*
> *I am God, and there is none like me.*
> *I make known the end from the beginning,*
> *from ancient times, what is still to come.*
> *I say, 'My purpose will stand,*
> *and <u>I will do all that I please</u>.'*
>
> Isaiah 46:10

Scripture abounds with accounts of God taking the initiative, telling man how it's going to be and then doing it. Here is Jesus announcing in plain terms what he intends to do to the church in Thyatira.

> *...but I have this against you, that you tolerate the woman Jezebel, who calls herself a prophetess, and she teaches and leads My bondservants astray so that they commit sexual immorality and eat things sacrificed to idols. I gave her time to repent, and she does not want to repent of her sexual immorality. Behold, I will throw her on a bed of sickness,*

> *and those who commit adultery with her into great tribulation, unless they repent of her deeds. And I will kill her children with plague, and all the churches will know that I am He who searches the minds and hearts; and I will give to each one of you according to your deeds.*
>
> Revelation 2:20-23

Who is talking? Jesus.

What's he going to do? Sickness, tribulation, plague.

Whose authority is he operating in? His own.

For the many scriptures depicting God's terrible, swift sword, however, there are other examples of God being talked out of taking action.

> *Then the Lord said to Moses, "I have seen this people, and behold, they are an obstinate people. So now leave Me alone, that My anger may burn against them and that I may destroy them.*
>
> *Then Moses pleaded with the Lord his God, and said, "Lord, why does Your anger burn against Your people whom You have brought out from the land of Egypt with great power and with a mighty hand? [. . .] Turn from Your burning anger and relent of doing harm to Your people.*
>
> *So the Lord relented of the harm which He said He would do.*
>
> Exodus 32:9-12, 14

We can note two things here. First, that God had the authority to act against the Children of Israel, and second, that he changed his mind when a man—who also had authority on the earth—talked him out of it. Yes, humans have authority. God expects us to use that authority. Ours is God-given authority. Meaning, it is intended to be used for godly purposes—redeemed men and women establishing God's kingdom on earth. Unredeemed men and women also have authority as human beings. They are establishing Satan's kingdom on earth. They may not know it, but when it comes crashing down and they see what takes its place, they'll know who did it.

GOD'S PROVISION

God relies on humans to carry out his will on earth. In that sense, God needs us. Rarely does anything on earth happen without the cooperation of humans. That is the power we have; that's how powerful we are. If God says A, and man says B, most times it's still B. And Jesus said, "Where two agree, it's two B (or not two B)."

We are the resource that God expects to use in advancing his kingdom. God will always look to man first and foremost.

This perspective throws religion into a tailspin. Religion needs to get thrown into a tailspin. That's what happens just before it crashes.

Here is an example of how God's provision works. What if God said to Fred (a totally random, made-up name), "Fred, I want you to give Greg a thousand dollars. He needs to hold a meeting in Texas."

Clearly, God wants Greg to have a thousand dollars. God promised to be Greg's resource for his assignment. But what happens if Fred says "No way! That guy's a bum!"

Well, does Greg still get the $1,000? Maybe. Maybe not.

Here are the possibilities.

- ➢ God gets somebody else with a totally made-up name to give Greg the $1,000.
- ➢ God gets the hotel to give Greg the meeting room for free.
- ➢ God tells Greg to cancel the meeting.
- ➢ Greg prays: "Hey God, maybe ask somebody with a real name for a change?"

The point is, we are the resource that God expects to use in advancing his kingdom. God will always look to man first and foremost.

ELIJAH'S PROVISION

In 1 Kings 19, Elijah was having a bad day. He had slaughtered the prophets of Baal and now was on the run from Jezebel, who apparently had not yet read of her fate in Revelation 2.

> *But he [Elijah] himself went a day's journey into the wilderness, and came and sat down under a broom tree; and he asked for himself to die, and said, "Enough! Now, Lord, take my life, for I am no better than my fathers." (v 4)*

God took direct action.

> *Then he [Elijah] lay down and fell asleep under a broom tree; but behold, there was an angel touching him, and he said to him, "Arise, eat!" And he looked, and behold, there was at his head a round loaf of bread baked on hot coals, and a pitcher of water. So he ate and drank, and lay down again. But the angel of the Lord came back a second time and touched him, and said, "Arise, eat; because the journey is too long for you." So he arose and ate and drank, and he journeyed in the strength of that food for forty days and forty nights to Horeb, the mountain of God. (v.5-8)*

Notice that no man was involved in restoring Elijah in this moment. He was at rock bottom. God had to intervene to save the life of this despondent prophet. But Elijah would not be allowed to remain in this condition. Having restored his body, God now restored his soul.

> *Then he came there to a cave and spent the night there; and behold, the word of the Lord came to him, and He said to him, "What are you doing here, Elijah?" (v. 9)*

Elijah pled his case.

> *I have been very zealous for the Lord.... And I alone am left; and they have sought to take my life. (v. 10)*

God's answer says it all. (It usually does.)

> *Yet I will leave seven thousand in Israel, all the knees that have not bowed to Baal and every mouth that has not kissed him. (v. 18)*

For all that Elijah faced—for all his suffering—God could have wiped out Jezebel, her gutless wimp of a husband Ahab, and the despicable prophets of Baal. But what would have changed? New Jezebels would have arisen from the children of men. New Ahabs would have been drawn to them and surrendered their...well, you know. And the demon Baal would have corrupted even more fools into becoming his prophets. The situation would have only grown worse, like cutting the stem of a weed but leaving the root.

Worst of all, Elijah would have failed the lesson. God wanted to work through him. Often, he is working the most when we think he is doing the least. Elijah thought he was alone, and indeed he was—alone in his cave. But standing where God stood, he was in good company—seven thousand strong—and well provided for.

And Fred? If you're still reading this, I'm waiting for that $1,000.

OUR PARTNERSHIP WITH GOD

Sometimes we do what we know God wants done. Who needs to hear from God before she feeds her children breakfast?

Sometimes we work hand in hand with God. *OK, God, how are we going to feed these children this morning?*

Sometimes God intervenes directly. "Hey, wake up. Your kids need fed. There's going to be a knock at the door."

Very little happens on earth without the cooperation of humans. That's the power we have. Without this understanding, we'll never mature into our ambassadorship in the earth. God's looking to partner with us, and he will go to great lengths to teach us this lesson. Sometimes, going without is the only way for us to get that lesson.

We pray and pray for God to provide, and we're still broke. We pray for healing, and we're still sick. We pray for neighborhoods, regions and nations, and they're still in darkness. We confess scriptures—the ones that support our viewpoint—and nothing comes to pass. Why?

Could it be that we've been waiting for God to do something, and God's waiting for us to do something? And what if that "something" looks like...oh, I don't know...work?

Take a deep breath. We are very important to God. If you are in a staring contest with God, you might as well blink first. He's good at waiting. He's eternal, you know. We are the ones who'll fall asleep someday.

THE PLAN

> *We've been waiting for God to do something, and God's waiting for us to do something.*

When Eve was about to pick the fruit from the tree of the knowledge of good and evil, why did God not stop her? He could have saved us all a lot of problems if he had just kept that woman from picking that fruit. Or...could he?

Fact is, God had a plan. He could have stopped Adam and Eve that day. But what about the next day, and the day after that? What would they have learned? We have to understand that God's reaction to Adam and Eve's disobedience was not damage control. The sentence of the devil, in the guise of a serpent, was swift and sure. And it heralded the Messiah.

And I will make enemies
Of you and the woman,
And of your offspring and her Descendant;
He shall bruise you on the head,
And you shall bruise Him on the heel.

Genesis 3:15

Recall the description of Jesus: "the Lamb who was slain from the creation of the world" (Revelation 13:8). Sure sounds like a plan, doesn't it? Hebrews carries through with this theme.

Therefore, when He comes into the world, He says,

"You have not desired sacrifice and offering,
But You have prepared a body for Me;
You have not taken pleasure in whole burnt offerings and offerings for sin.
Then I said, 'Behold, I have come
(It is written of Me in the scroll of the book)
To do Your will, O God.'"

The redemption of man was the whole plan of God. The Old Testament is the act of God fulfilling what he promised. God needed a body, so Jesus came into the earth.

The prophet Isaiah saw into this a little deeper.

Therefore the Lord Himself will give you a sign: Behold, the virgin will conceive and give birth to a son, and she will name Him Immanuel.

Isaiah 7:14

Interesting name, Immanuel. We traditionally interpret *Immanuel* as "God with us," but the *im* means "mankind." The *u-e-l* is *Elohim*, which means "God within a man." So the more accurate translation of Isaiah 4:17 is that a virgin is going to get pregnant and bring forth a son, and his name is going to be "God within a man's body."

For a Child will be born to us, a Son will be given to us.

Isaiah 9:6

Isaiah doesn't mean God's son would be *born*. Jesus was never born. The child was born; God's son was given. Don't confuse the child with the son. These are two different words, two different meanings of the Hebrew. Mary is not the mother of Jesus. Mary is the mother of the child. The child made the son a fully-vested human being. Jesus was fully man and fully God. Satan did not know what to do with that.

In Genesis 18, when God wanted to judge Sodom and Gomorrah, he could have simply wiped these cities off the map. Instead, God worked through Abraham to release his judgment in the earth. Abraham begged God for mercy. God was still sovereign, and Abraham's entreaties were just that: appeals. In the end, God granted Abraham leeway, but ten righteous individuals could not be found, so God carried out his judgment with the explicit acknowledgement of the reigning man.

> *The redemption of man was the whole plan of God. The Old Testament is the act of God fulfilling what he promised.*

Then the Lord God formed the man of dust from the ground and breathed into his nostrils the breath of life; and the man became a living person.

Genesis 2:7

When God created man, the *humas*-man, he put his nostrils to man's nostrils and breathed life. This was echoed in the Gospels. After his crucifixion, Jesus sat on the bank of the sea and fixed breakfast for his disciples. Then he did something profound:

And when He had said this, He breathed on them and said to them, "Receive the Holy Spirit.

John 20:22

In the Greek and in the Hebrew, the definition is the same. It's the same breathing. He imparted Holy Spirit to them at that beach. They were able to receive the governor of the earth back into their life. Holy Spirit was able to come. Then He said, "Go to the upper room and wait for the promise."

The promise of what?

Holy Spirit.

I thought they just got the Holy Spirit when he breathed on them.

The beach was the impartation. The upper room was the activation. It was the manifestation of Holy Spirit in their lives that they received.

Then on Pentecost, they did things they could never have done on their own. They spoke in other tongues—tongues of flames. Peter preached like a man on fire and 3,000 souls were added to the kingdom.

THE LAW OF PRAYER

The legal authority on earth is in the hands of humans (*humas-man*). We have authority. Although God is sovereign, he rarely violates this arrangement. Very little happens on earth without mankind's cooperation. This is why God desires us to pray, petition, and partner with him.

> *Whatever you bind on earth shall have been bound in heaven.*
>
> Matthew 18:18
>
> *That men ought always to pray.*
>
> Luke 18:1
>
> *If two of you agree on earth about anything that they may ask, it shall be done for them by My Father who is in heaven.*
>
> Matthew 18:19

Mankind holds the license on the earth. God is the licensor—the one who issued the license. Jesus still retains ultimate authority on earth. We obtain authority through our citizenship according to the kingdom.

> *Jesus [said], "All authority has been given to Me in heaven and on earth. Go therefore and make disciples of all the nations, baptizing them in the name of the Father and the Son and the Holy Spirit, teaching them to observe all that I commanded you; and lo, I am with you always, even to the end of the age."*
>
> Matthew 28:18-20

10

Conclusion

IN THE BEGINNING, a dormant body lay lifeless and empty, an unfinished work of vast potential. Created by God, it awaited its creator's words to bring it to life. As the Spirit of God hovered over the surface of the deep, the Creator spoke: "Light be!" And light was. So, life began on the nascent being we call earth—our home planet.

In time, another dormant body lay lifeless. Created by God, it also awaited its creator's word to bring it to life. Crafted from the dust of the earth—the dirt—it resembled a man but was not yet a man until the Creator infused it with the breath of life. Thus, the man became a living soul.

The man emerged into life and learned of his mission. He was given dominion—*radah*—over the earth. He was also given a partner, one from his own body. She was not created from dirt, but from flesh and bone. Together, they ruled as king and queen under the sovereignty of the Lord.

They were well equipped to rule all of creation. They had bodies, souls and spirits. They were capable, adaptable and young. When they reached for the knowledge of good and evil, however, they lost more than their innocence. They lost their right to rule. The kingdom passed from man to Satan. As a result, sin (rebellion, treason) entered the world, and death spread to all who would come after them because all men sinned.

Yet God had a plan. Some suspect it was his plan all along.

A third lifeless body lay dormant. Sent by the Father, he was both son of God and son of man. He came to reestablish the government of the kingdom, and his task was nearly complete. He built his ekklesia, and the gates of hell could not prevail against it. He appointed ambassadors, citizens of his kingdom, to go into the world bearing the power and authority of the Kingdom of God. He opened the heavens for the Spirit of God—the same spirit that once brooded over the dark planet—to fill believers everywhere. He left a testament forged in the blood of his sacrifice. Being the very word of God, he rose to life, and his life was the light of mankind.

> *Yet God had a plan. Some suspect it was his plan all along.*

Today, another body lies dormant. It resembles what God intended; but it is unfinished, a lifeless form, powerless and ineffective. Trouble is, it doesn't know it's dormant. It believes it is God's kingdom on earth, yet it is a kingdom of ritual, doctrine, hierarchy and grandiose observances. Stone statues are kissed to receive a blessing. Saints of old are prayed to as intermediaries to the Father. A hierarchy of titled men and women purport to search the scriptures on behalf of the masses, but they never arrive at the living Christ framed within these anointed words.

We live in a time when death masquerades as life, when lies are deemed truth, and darkness prevails over light. God's people are being systematically destroyed for a lack of knowledge. And who is the destroyer? The same who parades himself as the god of this world. Satan's reign is over; Jesus ended it. Yet not everyone realizes this.

After the Civil War of America, battles were still being fought weeks after Lee's surrender at Appomattox. News traveled slowly in

Conclusion

the 1800s. Peace had been won, but the news of that peace had yet to reach the population.

Today, we stand on the brink of fully realizing the kingdom that Jesus won over 2,000 years ago. Even in our age of information, news travels slowly, yet all the powers of darkness cannot stop it from spreading. Our message is sure and our success is guaranteed...if we participate.

> *We are called, equipped, and destined. It is time to stand.*

Interesting word, *guaranteed.* People associate it with many other qualities: *safe, easy, simple, a slam dunk.* With regard to the Kingdom of God, its prevalence is assured. Victory has already been won. What is not certain is how that victory will manifest.

How many good people will suffer? How many innocent people will die? How many evil people will be exalted until we—the church—take our rightful place in the Kingdom of God as citizens: sons and daughters of the King?

When God breathed life into the earth, into mankind, and into his very son, he could only initiate life. The will to live, to go forth and accomplish all that the Creator desired, had to arise from an inherent drive. This also came through God's word. The earth was commissioned. Mankind was commissioned. Even Jesus was commissioned. And they responded with vigor.

Today, we are in a war for the furtherance of God's purpose. The needs are all around us. The fields are white with harvest, and there's territory to be taken. We are called sons and daughters, kings and queens, but for what purpose? A place at the table? Royal privilege? A gilded throne? No. We are endowed with rights to fulfill our commission. We each have a calling and a free will. We are appointed citizen ambassadors of the Kingdom of God to establish God's kingdom. We have a job to do.

Yes, we have certain rights and responsibilities...yet we also have a choice. Will we fulfill our destiny? Or will we merely clutch our ticket to heaven and count the days until our release from this mortal veil? Will we join the fight? Or is our salvation only about our lives and not the lives of many?

Our purpose is not simply about leaving this planet of darkness; it is about taking the nations for our King. It is about being the light.

Karl Marx, father of modern communism, famously said: "Religion is the opiate of the masses." He was right. It is. Mere religion pacifies us, sedates us, distracts us from the real objective and occupies us with form over function. Religion is addictive. It works by triggering our response to a challenge. We hear "Study to show yourself approved," and we act as if we're told: "Work hard to earn God's favor." We substitute the efforts of blind men for the infusion of God's illuminating Spirit. In truth, we are human beings, called to rule and reign. We are called, equipped and destined. It is time to stand.

God's kingdom is rising from the grip of religion. God has breathed life into it. Rest assured; the Kingdom of God will fill the earth.

> *At the name of Jesus every knee will bow, of those who are in heaven and on earth and under the earth, and that every tongue will confess that Jesus Christ is Lord, to the glory of God the Father.*
>
> Philippians 2:10-11

What is the message? We will bow, or we will perish. Scripture assures us that the gifts and calling of God are without repentance. The participation of each of us, however, is not assured.

Our choice is simple. Rise up and join the living. Or shrink back and fade into obscurity. Let us not be manipulated with tales of hell and outer darkness; God holds the keys to those realms, and his judgment is sure. Rather, let us acknowledge something greater: the call of destiny and the relentless draw of our place in God's government.

Conclusion

As citizens of God's Kingdom, let us rise and stand in our appointed place in the seen and unseen realms as God's great plan fills the earth. It is coming. It is here. It is forever.

> *I think over again my small adventures,*
> *... My fears,*
> *Those small ones that seemed so big.*
> *For all the vital things I had to get and to reach.*
> *And yet there is only one great thing,*
> *The only thing.*
> *To live to see the great day that dawns*
> *And the light that fills the world.*
>
> Ancient Song

PRAYER

Father, I pray for a mighty shift in the lives of your fellow kingdom citizens. Shift them out of the ways and influence of religion, and into your stronghold of citizenship. Holy Spirit, move them into a deeper understanding of who they are in you and the power you are in their lives. Make them dangerous on the earth. Cause darkness to be driven back and the kingdoms of this world to bow their knees to you because of the efforts of your sons and daughters. Strengthen, encourage and activate them for a greater kingdom purpose. In Jesus' Strong Name! Amen!

I decree that you are becoming more aware of who you are as a citizen in God's kingdom, and that your citizenship translates into a greater release of your ambassadorship so that the influence that Father has set you in will began to look like heaven (ref. Matthew 6:10).

About the Author

GREG HOOD WAS BORN AND RAISED IN AMORY, MISSISSIPPI, and has been in ministry for over 37 years. He is the President and Founder of Greg Hood Ministries, The Network of Five-Fold Ministers and Churches, as well as Kingdom University. All are based in the United States of America. He is the lead apostle at Kingdom Life Ekklesia in Franklin, TN, which he and Joan established in late 2021.

Greg apostolically leads many leaders and churches around the globe. He is a planter of apostolic centers and has pioneered several apostolic centers within the United States and in other parts of the world. Greg travels extensively, empowering believers to passionately pursue their God-given mandate, resulting in personal and societal transformation. His greatest passion is to see the Body of Christ come to its fullness within the Kingdom of God. Greg is driven with great passion to speak into the lives of those who are called into leadership to the Church, Government, and the Marketplace. He burns to see people become whom God has fashioned them to be.

Greg attended Christ for the Nations Institute in Dallas, Texas, from 1987-1988. He received his Master of Theology in 2006 and his Doctor of Theology in 2008 from Kairos Bible Training Center in Waco, Texas.

Greg has authored several other books, including Rebuilding the Broken Altar; Awakening out of Chaos in 2020, The Gospel of the Kingdom in 2022, and Sonship According to the Kingdom; Steeping into the Power of True Identity in 2023. These books are also in other languages.

Greg and his wife, Joan, have been married for 27 years. The Hoods base their ministry headquarters in Franklin, Tennessee.

Contact Information
Dr. Greg Hood, Th.D.
Greg Hood Ministries / Kingdom University
1113 Murfreesboro Road
Suite 106 #222
Franklin, TN 37064
office@greghood.org
www.GregHood.org
www.KingdomU.org

Previous Work

Praise for: *Sonship According to the Kingdom*

Sadly, many believers never come to a true understanding of who they really are in Christ. Paul rebuked the Corinthians for acting like mere humans. We are more than saved sinners; we are new creations. As sons and daughters of the Most High God, we're filled with His Spirit, infused with His nature, heirs in His kingdom, and partners in His great cause. You *will* come to a greater revelation of this as you read Greg Hood's powerful book *Sonship According to the Kingdom*.

Dr. Dutch Sheets
Dutch Sheets Ministries and *Give Him 15* daily prayer and decrees.
Bestselling author of: *Authority in Prayer, An Appeal to Heaven, Intercessory Prayer*

As I ponder on Jewels in the Lord's Treasury, that at times have been lost and must be rediscovered, I am drawn to three words that start with the Letter "I." These are not just catchy words or phrases, but rather character traits. These are: 1) Integrity... 2) Intensity... and 3) Identity... It would easy for me to add in some of my other favorite Kingdom "I" Words such as "Intercession" and "Intentionally" and others.

I have the honor of endorsing Dr. Greg Hood's book, *Sonship According to the Kingdom*.

Equipped to Be An Equipper!

Dr. James W Goll
God Encounters Ministries, GOLL Ideation LLC

Nations are in a crisis driven largely by the curse of fatherlessness and the breakdown of the nuclear family unit. The solution: reversing the curse through *Sonship According to the Kingdom*. We belong. We are His. We are not forsaken. We are not orphans. He has taken fatherhood responsibility for us. This powerful book, penned by my friend Greg Hood, holds the keys not just for a transformed life but for the power to change the world!

Jane Hamon
Apostle, Vision Church @ Christian International
Author: *Dreams and Visions, The Deborah Company, The Cyrus Decree, Discernment and Declarations for Breakthrough*

Sonship According to the Kingdom takes the reader on a thoughtful journey through what it means to be a child of God. Greg Hood demonstrates a passion to see people live life to the fullest. To do so, he points out, we must understand the resources at our disposal. Gone are the days when Christians can rationalize away a weak faith. *Sonship According to the Kingdom* challenges the reader to see tangible evidence of a life devoted to Christ. Those content with a mediocre lifestyle need not read this book.

Christina Bobb
Attorney for President Donald J. Trump
Author, *Stealing Your Vote: The Inside Story of the 2020 Election and What It Means for 2024*

Functioning in the miraculous power of the Lord, walking through test and trials and/or being used to impact the world with the kingdom of God requires essentially one thing. That thing is a revelation of who we are as the sons of God. When we, by the revelation of the Spirit of God, recognize our status with God, rejection vanishes and empowerment comes. My longtime friend, Greg Hood, does a masterful job of highlighting these truths in his new book *Sonship According to the Kingdom*. You will not be disappointed in your investment of this book. It could change your life!

Robert   Henderson
Best-Selling Author of *The Courts of Heaven* series

In the 1500-year-old classic book by Sun Tzu: *The Art of War*, we are reminded that for victory, "one must know their enemy...many fail to see that for victory, one must know themselves...." Dr. Greg Hood has hit the mark in his new book *Sonship According to the Kingdom*. He declares forcefully the importance of Kingdom believers embracing and living out their new identity in Christ. This powerful volume will unleash Kingdom potential in all who grasp its powerful truths....

Dr. Ron Phillips, D. Min
Pastor Emeritus Abba's House, Chattanooga, TN
Fresh Oil Ministries

Citizenship According to the Kingdom

This book is a must-read! I was informed, enlightened, and impacted as I devoured the pages of this well-written and very understandable volume!

I love the way Greg wove together a tapestry of Biblical, theological, historical, and autobiographical strands to present the revelation of the Kingdom of God, and its expression and ministry, in the earth through the sons and daughters of the Lord God. There are many places in the book where you will laugh as you are learning.

The heart of this book will assist the followers of King Jesus to be prepared for life and ministry as each one sees his or her identity as a son or a daughter of Father God and a member of His family.

Dr. Jim Hodges
Federation of Ministers and Churches International
Cedar Hill, TX

Previous Work

Praise for: *The Gospel of the Kingdom.*

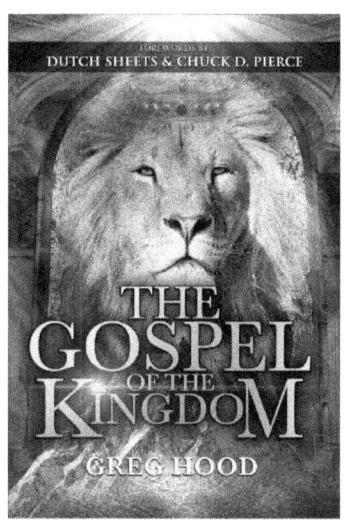

My friend, Greg Hood, is not only a teacher of the Word, but he is a student. Ever learning, ever maturing...as we all should be. The concepts and truth in this book may be new to you and that's okay. They are based on Scripture yet are just coming into their season. Kingdom, Kingdom Connection, Ekklesia, Apostles, Reigning in Life and so much more within these pages that will inspire you and encourage you and above all, change you. I encourage you to grab a cup of coffee, open your hearts and minds to what God is saying and doing, and take notes! Get ready to grow.

Tim Sheets, Apostle
Author of *Angel Armies, Angel Armies on Assignment, Planting the Heavens*
Tim Sheets Ministries
The Oasis Church, Middletown, Ohio

In *The Gospel of the Kingdom,* my friend Greg Hood gives us language that stirs our hearts with a fresh passion to see God's governmental rule manifested in the earth. This book will help develop in you a heart for that which God Himself is passionate about. Let it stir you with that which stirs Him, the redemption of all things back to Himself.

Robert Henderson
Best-Selling Author, *Courts of Heaven Series*

The Gospel of the Kingdom will revolutionize how believers live out the mission and mandate of Christ to change our world. Apostle Greg Hood brings a fresh approach to this vital topic which will empower members of Christ's Ekklesia to use their God given authority to cause God's Kingdom to come & will to be done on earth as it is in heaven.

Jane Hamon, Apostle
Vision Church

Apostolic and Prophetic voices everywhere agree that the church, the ekklesia, has shifted into a new age, a new Reformation. In his book, *The Gospel of the Kingdom*, Dr. Greg Hood challenges believers to shift out of a mindset of practicing a religion into one of fulfilling God's original Kingdom mandate to redeem and restore the earth. As God's earthly ambassadors of His Kingdom, we must grasp the authority and responsibility invested in us, and to examine scripture in a fresh light and understanding so that we can cause the kingdoms of this world to become the kingdoms of our Lord and of his Christ.

Tom Hamon, Apostle
Vision Church

Previous Work

Dr. Greg Hood has written a very necessary book for the body of Christ at this critical time. It is an apostolic foundation for us to stand upon and will give context and order to our Kingdom call. *The Gospel of the Kingdom* has been written by a scholar who loves the word of God and has communicated in a fresh and direct way exactly what the Lord was sent by the Father to do and why we are being equipped, "For such a time as this." the Kingdom assignments that are before us will require binding the strongman and plundering the enemy.

Anne S. Tate
International Director of Prayer and the Watches
Glory of Zion, International

The Gospel of the Kingdom is one of the most important messages that undergirds much of our understanding of Scripture and the relationship between man and God. Jesus who was a perfect man and God incarnate made the Gospel of the Kingdom the essence of his preaching while he was on earth making the Gospel of the Kingdom the most important message Jesus ever preached and that he expects his followers all over the world to emulate. I am convinced that much of the body of Christ is weak because of a lack of understanding of the Gospel of the Kingdom. My dear friend Dr. Greg Hood's book completely changes that unfortunate trajectory by reintroducing much of the body of Christ to the Gospel of the Kingdom. I highly recommend this powerful book for anyone who is serious about personal transformation and the transformation of culture.

Dr. Francis Myles
Author: *The Order of Melchizedek*
Founder: Francis Myles International

THIS BOOK! Here it is, an astoundingly simple yet profound picture of the Kingdom of God. Greg does such a great job of bringing the truth out about God's original intention, what He had in mind to do, from "...before the foundation of the world." This book clears up all the questionable things we have heard and been taught regarding His will, His character, His heart for humanity and His Kingdom purpose. It's a MUST-READ!

Apostle Randy Lopshire
Riverside Church
Clarksville, TN

My family and I have gotten to know Greg and Joan Hood, not only in a spiritual leadership way, but also in a personal way.

They are true, kind and wise ... beyond their years

This book is an amazing read. Greg's wisdom and interpretation of scripture is so insightful and energizing! Everyone needs a copy of this book as a guideline for life and salvation! We are proud to know and love this man of God and have the utmost confidence in him.

Shalom to all!
Lily Isaacs and the Isaacs Family
Members of the Grand Ole Opry

Previous Work

Praise for *Rebuilding the Broken Altar – Awakening Out of Chaos.*

This book is as loaded with keen insight and Spirit-inspired revelation as any you will find. You would be hard pressed to find a book more timely and more relevant for the Church and the nations—especially America—than Rebuilding the Broken Altar. Sadly, many books simply restate others' teachings, simply coloring them with a different spin. However, it is refreshing when I read a book that feeds me new thoughts and information. Simply stated, I was more than entertained and inspired by Greg's book—I learned a lot!

Dr. Dutch Sheets, Dutch Sheets Ministries and Give Him 15 daily prayer and decrees.
Bestselling author of: *Authority in Prayer, An Appeal to Heaven, Intercessory Prayer*

IF THERE WAS EVER A TIME WHEN a people needed to return to the Lord it is now. In his book "Rebuilding the Broken Altar" Greg Hood gives insight to the necessary process of recovering ourselves from the snare of the devil and experiencing the blessing of God again as a people. I would encourage, as you read to allow the Holy Spirit to stir your heart again with His passion for us individually and as a nation.

Robert Henderson
Best Selling Author of *The Courts of Heaven Series*

In *Rebuilding the Broken Altar*, Greg Hood presents a masterpiece of hope for the future of the church, for America and for nations crying out for a move of God. He carefully, Biblically and prophetically lays out a blueprint for revival that every leader and believer alike can work with to shift culture and engage the spiritual atmosphere to bring change. The word studies bring incredible insight and reveal the important elements necessary for rebuilding the altar of the Lord which has been broken down in both the church and in society in order to see an unprecedented outpouring from heaven, for harvest and transformation.

Dr. Jane Hamon, Vision Church @ Christian International
Author of: *Dreams and Visions, The Deborah Company, The Cyrus Decree, Discernment*

My friend Greg Hood is known as hard-hitting, straight-shooting and uncompromising in his preaching. His writing is even more so! I love the way he boldly challenges us to break free from old religious mindsets so that we can embrace God's kingdom plans. In his new book *Rebuilding the Broken Altar*, Greg gives us a clear vision of a restored church. With rich insights about the twelve tribes of Israel,

Previous Work

he takes us on a journey toward the restoration of New Testament faith. You will be challenged and inspired!

J. Lee Grady, Author and Director of The Mordecai Project

Dr. Greg Hood helps us to understand the meaning of the time and grasp the seismic impact of the altar. I have had the privilege of Greg's friendship and the blessings of his clear prophetic voices. I praise the Lord Jesus for enabling him to write this valuable book.

Tamrat Layne, Former Prime Minister, Ethiopia

The bottom-line message of this book, God is not finished with you or America, but the church and some pastors and some of us in government need to get our stones together.

Rep. Gene Ward, PhD, Hawai'i House of Representatives

Kingdom University

<u>KINGDOM UNIVERSITY</u> offers accredited and degreed classes in:

- Christian Counseling
- Kingdom Studies
- Business
- Five-Fold Ministry
- Government Studies
- The Arts

<u>CAMPUSES IN:</u>

- Georgia
- Indiana
- Louisiana
- Missouri
- North Carolina
- Texas
- Illinois
- Kentucky
- Mississippi
- New Jersey
- Tennessee
- Online Campus

More campuses coming to a state near you!

<u>INSTRUCTORS INCLUDE:</u>

Dr. Greg Hood	Dr. Ron Phillips	Apostle Tommy Kelly
Dr. Dutch Sheets	Dr. Tod Zeiger	Apostle Bob Long
Dr. Tim Sheets	Dr. Tom Schlueter	Apostle Jacquie Tyre
Dr. Jane Hamon	Dr. Alemu Beeftu	Apostle Regina Shank
Dr. Tom Hamon	Dr. Scott Reece	Apostle Kerry Kirkwood
Dr. Dwain Miller		

Kingdom University meets one weekend a month on a Friday evening and a Saturday. School year is from January-November. (We do not have classes in July and December.)

Register today by going to: www.KingdomU.org
Contact us at: Office@KingdomU.org

WE WILL SEE YOU IN THE CLASS ROOM!

www.ingramcontent.com/pod-product-compliance
Lightning Source LLC
Chambersburg PA
CBHW060655100426
42734CB00047B/1799